DOLLAR BILL ORIGAMI

Model designs by Won Park
Illustrations and instructions by Marcio Noguchi

STERLING INNOVATION
New York

An Imprint of Sterling Publishing Co., Inc.
1166 Avenue of the Americas
New York, NY 10036

ISBN: 978-1-4351-5252-6

This book is part of the *Dollar Bill Origami* kit and is not to be sold separately.

For information about custom editions, special sales, and premium and corporate purchases, please contact Sterling Special Sales at 800-805-5489 or specialsales@sterlingpublishing.com.

Manufactured in China

6 8 10 9 7 5

sterlingpublishing.com

Developed by The Book Shop, Ltd.
Model designs by Won Park
Illustrations and instructions by Marcio Noguchi
Book and box designed by Tim Palin Creative
Photography by Andrew Werner Photography

CONTENTS

SYMBOLS

Edge

Existing crease

Valley fold

Mountain fold

Fold in front

Fold behind

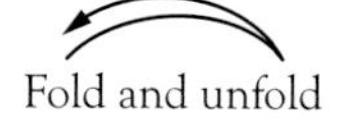

Fold and unfold

Hidden lines

Rotate

Sink / Squash / Push

View from here

Turn over

Open

9–14

Repeat steps on this side

Magnify

Close up detail next

Pleat

BASIC FOLDS AND BASES

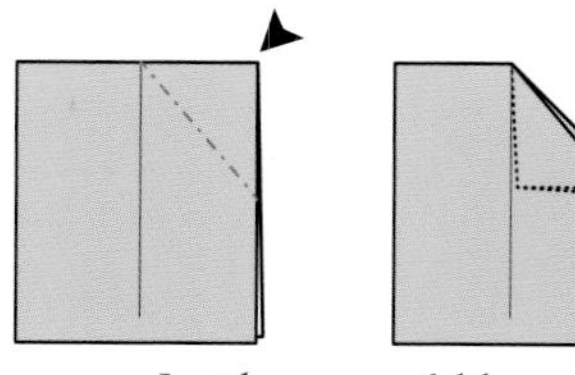

Inside reverse fold

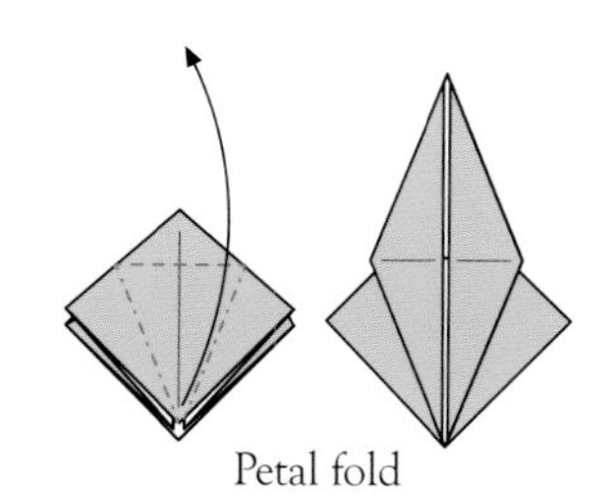

Petal fold

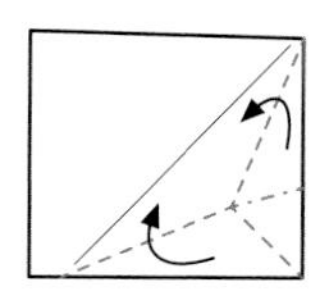

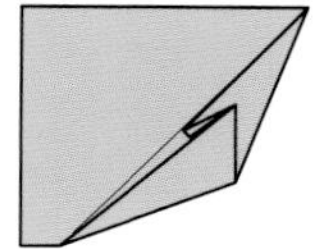

Rabbit-ear fold

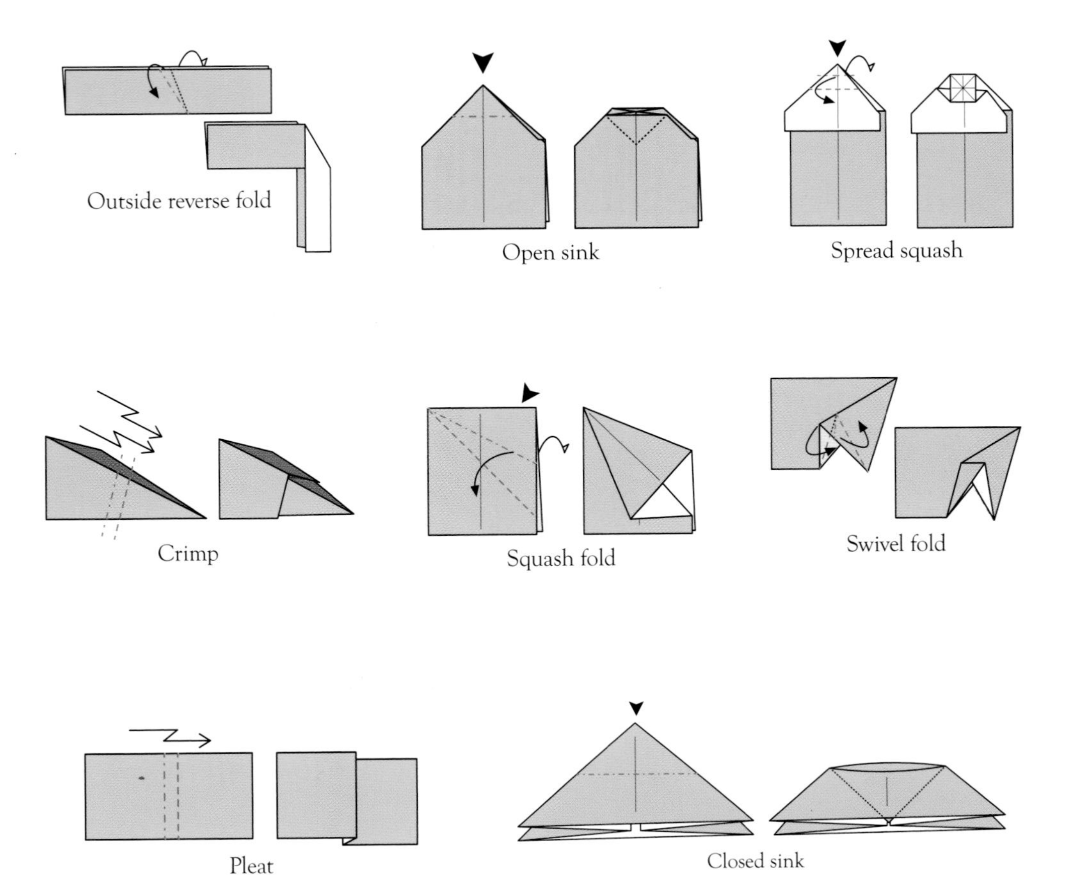
Outside reverse fold
Open sink
Spread squash
Crimp
Squash fold
Swivel fold
Pleat
Closed sink

RING

This model cannot be made with the practice currency in this kit because the insignia on the front of the ring requires the crest that appears on the front of a real dollar bill. Start with the green (back) side up so that the ring's "stone" centers precisely over the eagle emblem.

1 Fold the bill in half horizontally. Unfold.

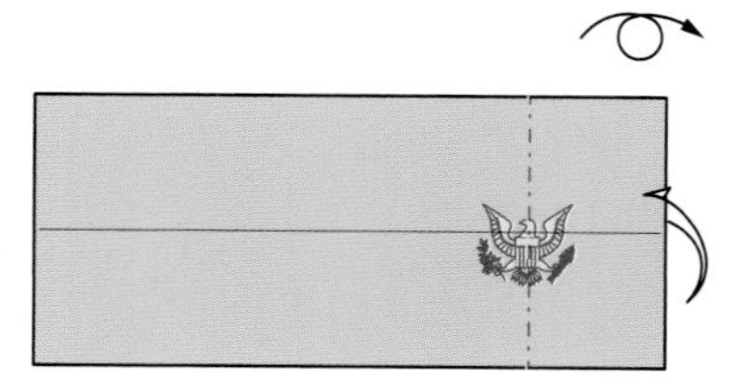

2 Make a mountain crease through the center of the eagle. The crease should align with the point at the bottom of the shield and the eagle's center tail feather. Turn over from top to bottom.

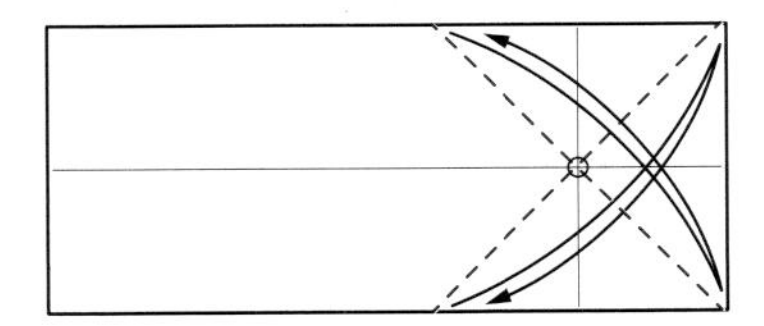

3 Valley fold the diagonals as indicated. Unfold.

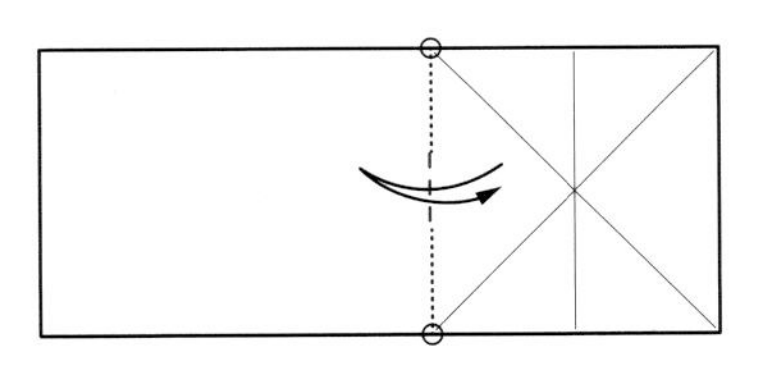

4 Create a pinch mark at the center crease as indicated.

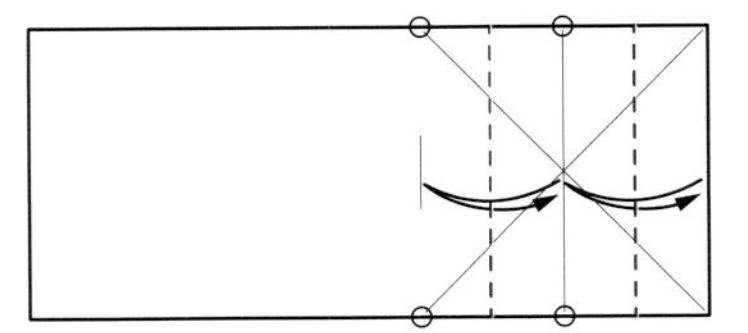

5 Valley fold as indicated, edge to crease mark and crease to crease mark. Unfold.

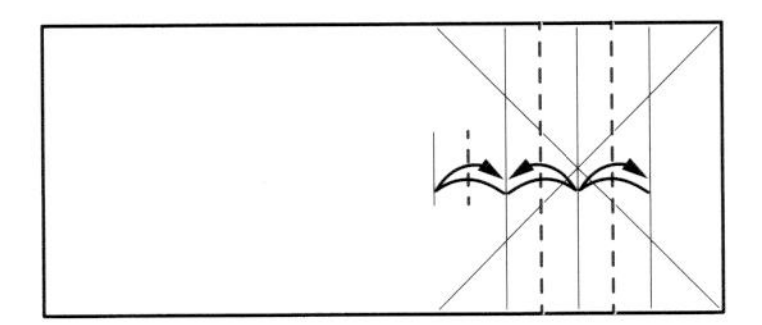

6 Crease between the creases. Unfold.

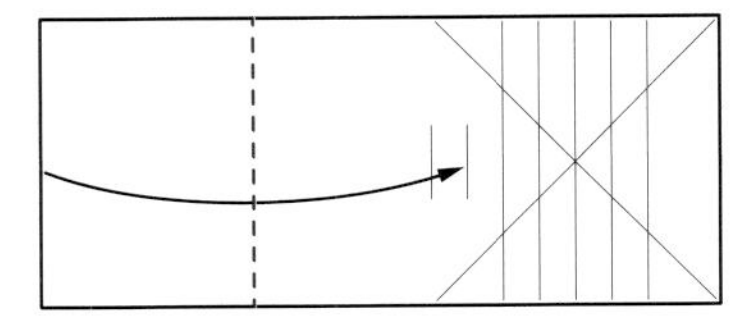

7 Fold the edge to the crease mark shown.

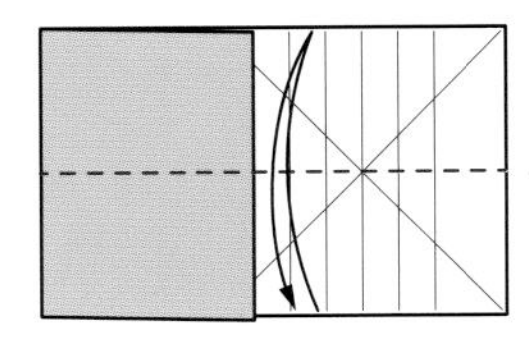

8 Fold the bottom edge to the top edge. Unfold.

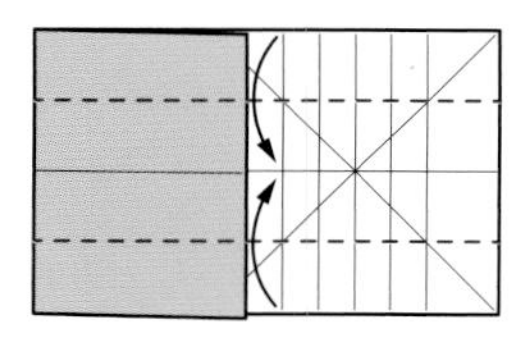

9 Fold the edges to the center.

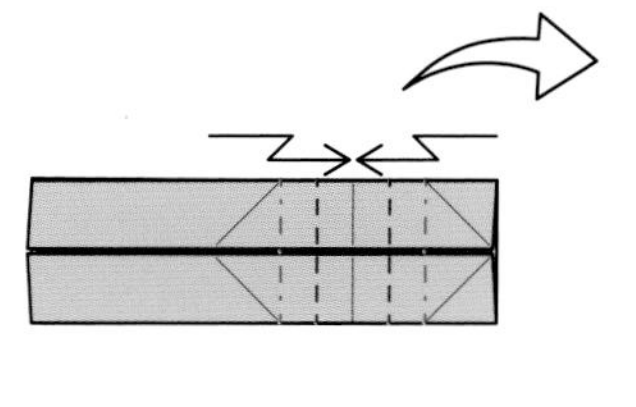

10 Pleat on existing creases.

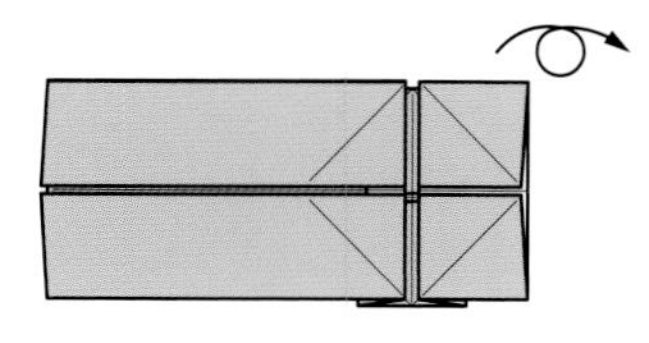

11 Turn over.

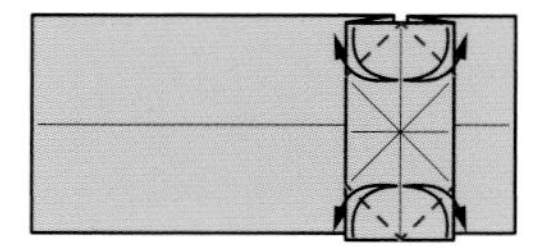

12 Fold the corners to the center crease and unfold.

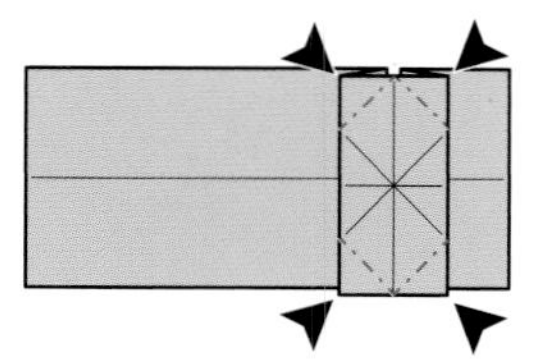

13 Reverse fold the corners on the creases made in step 12.

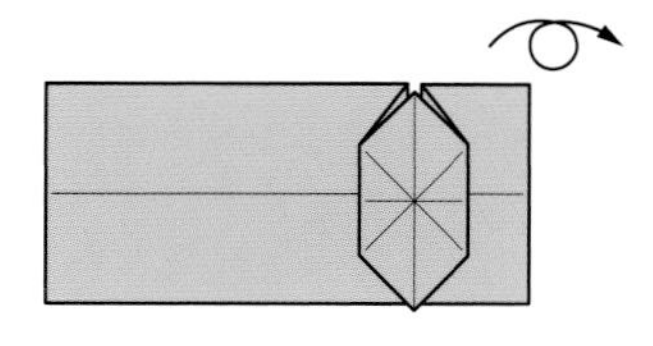

14 Turn over.

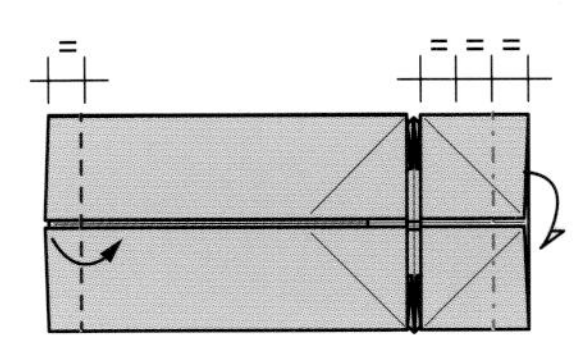

15 Fold the edges as indicated. Mountain fold at about ⅓ of the distance between the right edge and the crease. Valley fold the same width on the left edge.

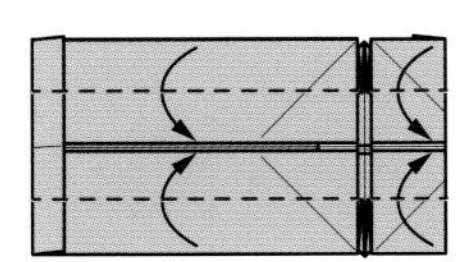

16 Fold the top and bottom edges to the center.

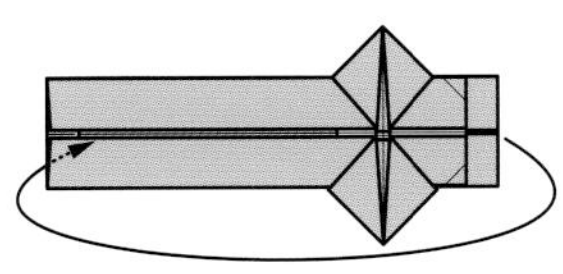

17 Curl the paper into a ring shape and insert the folded edge on the short end into the pocket formed by the layers on the long end.

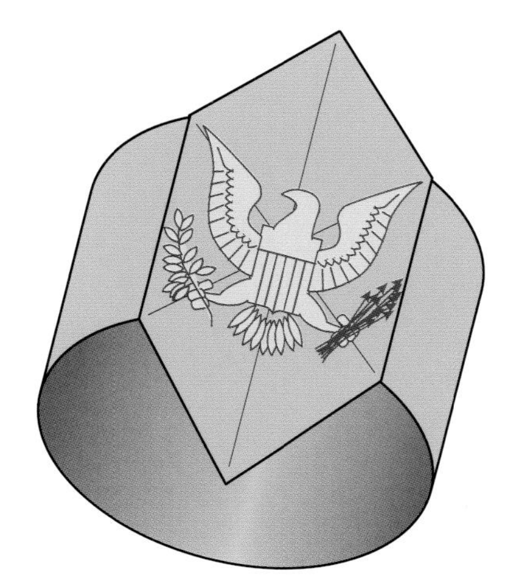

The completed ring

DRESS

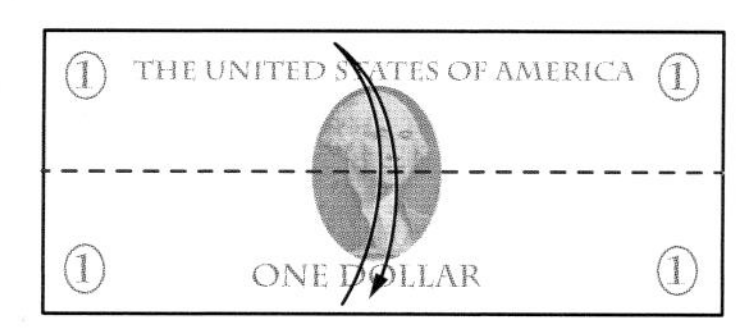

1 Start with the white (face) side up. Valley fold in half. Unfold.

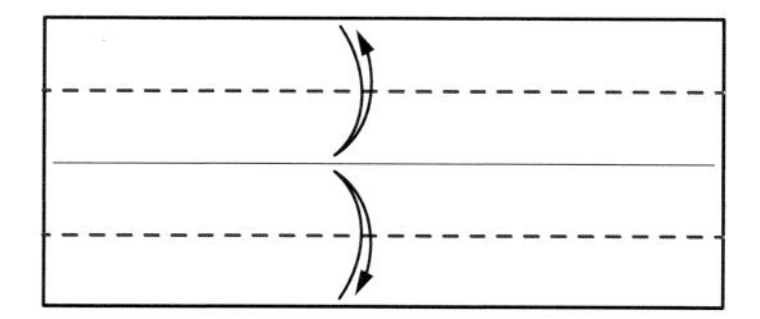

2 Valley fold in quarters. Unfold.

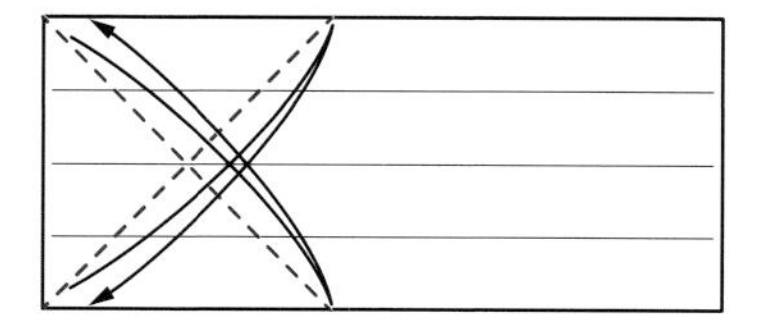

3 Valley fold the diagonals. Unfold.

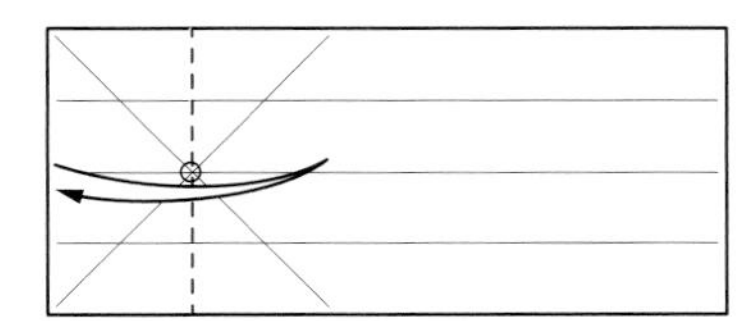

4 Crease vertically through the intersection point indicated.

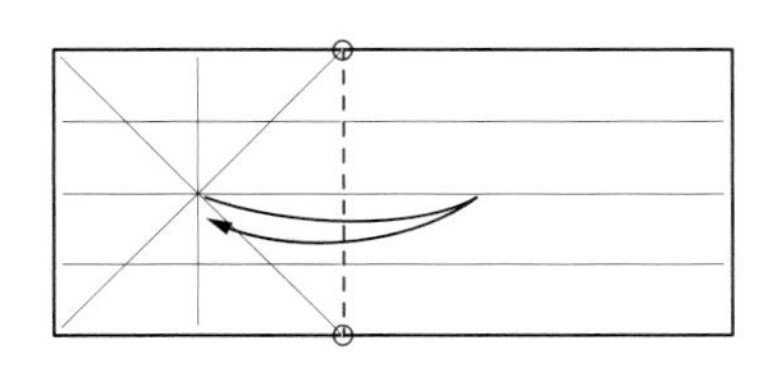

5 Crease between the points indicated.

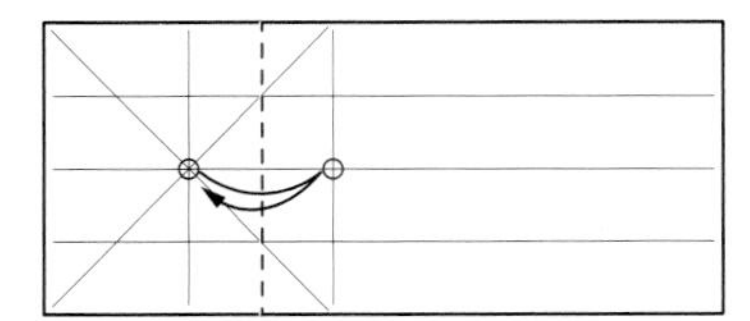

6 Fold between the crease lines. Unfold.

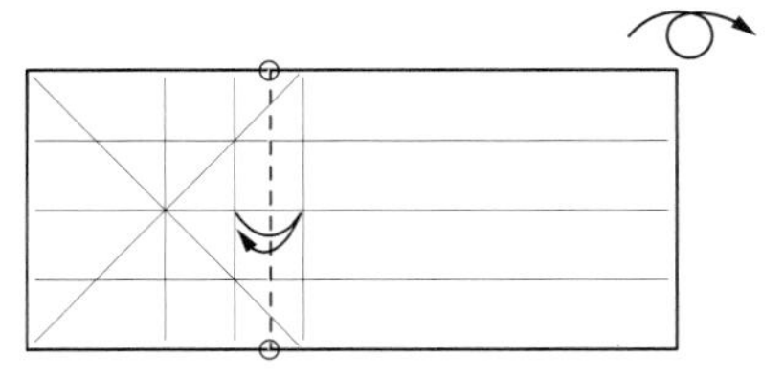

7 Fold between the crease lines. Unfold. Turn over from top to bottom.

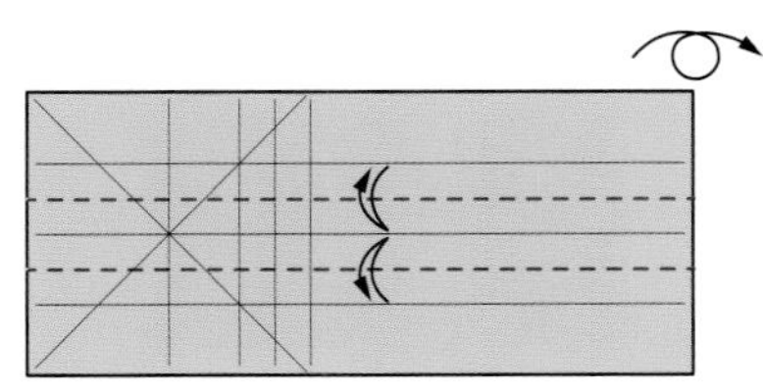

8 Fold between the crease lines. Unfold. Turn over from top to bottom.

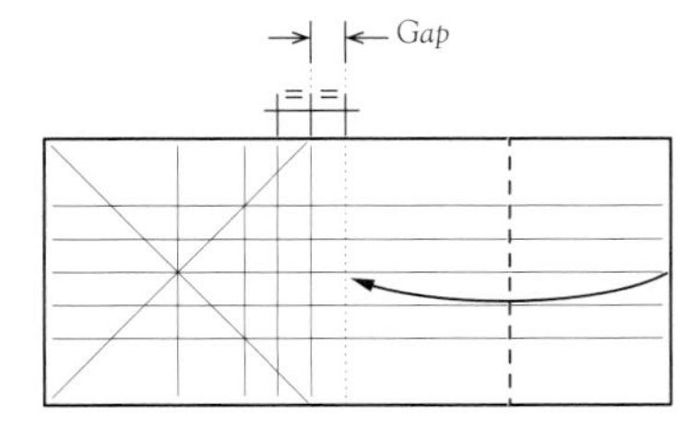

9 Fold as indicated, leaving a small gap between the edge and the crease line.

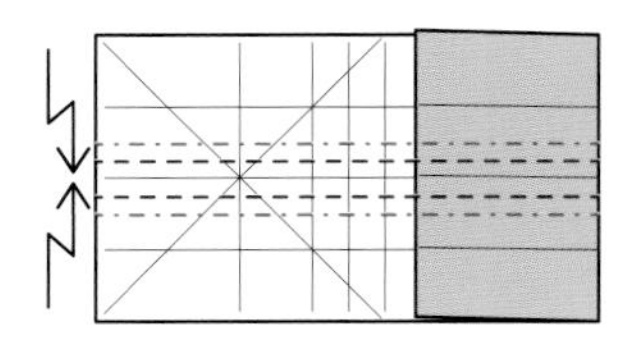

10 Pleat: Valley and mountain fold as shown, bringing the mountain edges to the center.

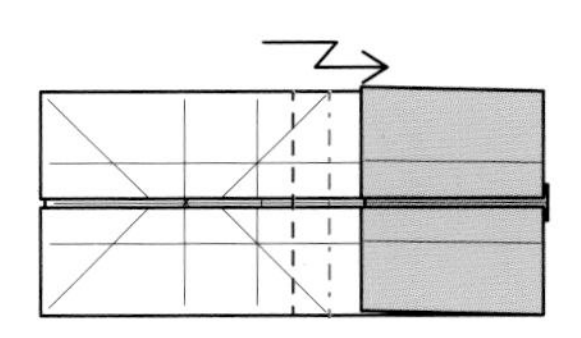

11 Pleat on existing creases.

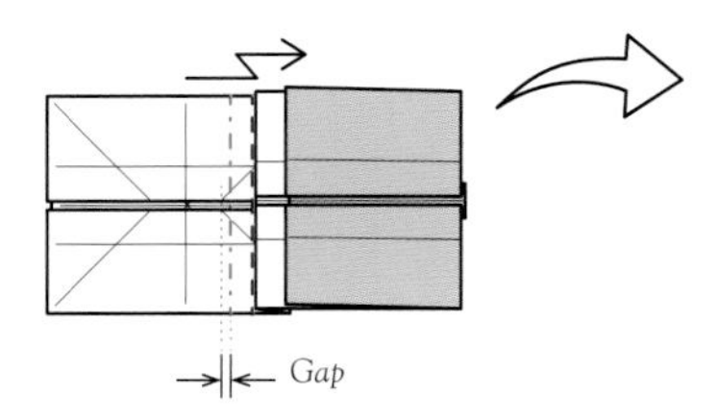

12 Create a smaller pleat, leaving a little gap between the new pleat and the previous one.

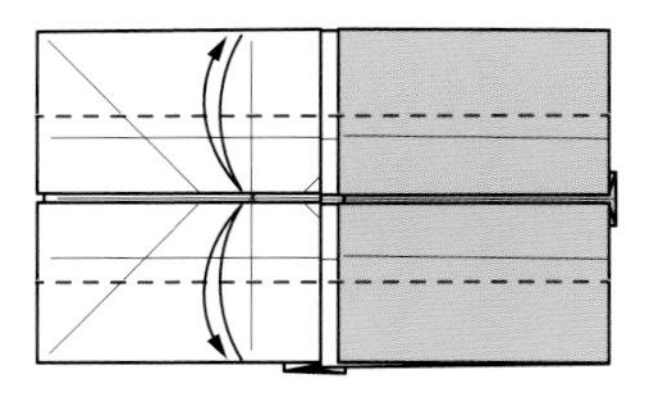

13 Fold the edges to the center. Unfold.

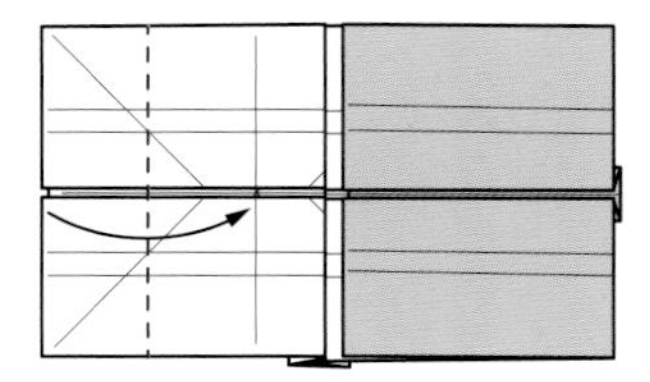

14 Fold the edge to the crease.

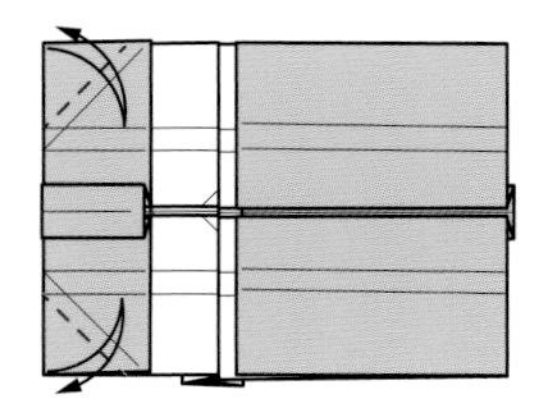

15 Fold the corners to the creases shown to form angle bisectors. Unfold.

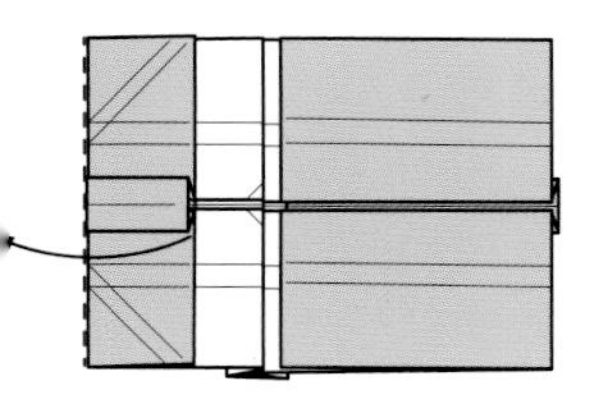

16 Unfold the flap.

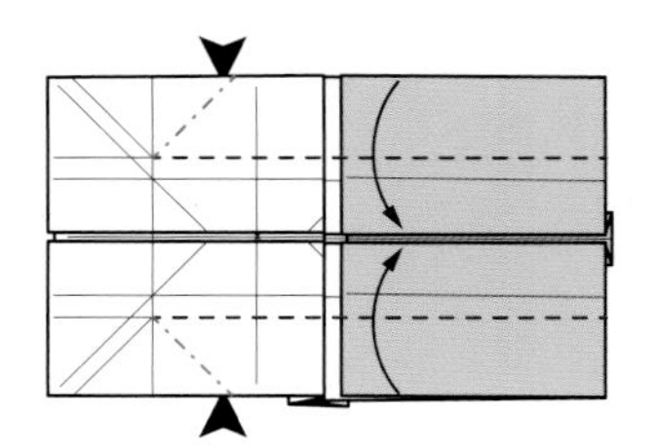

17 Collapse, using the creases indicated. Note: the model will not lie flat.

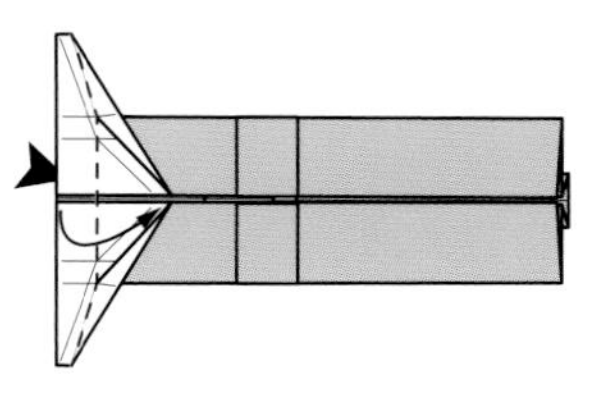

18 Fold flat, using the creases indicated.

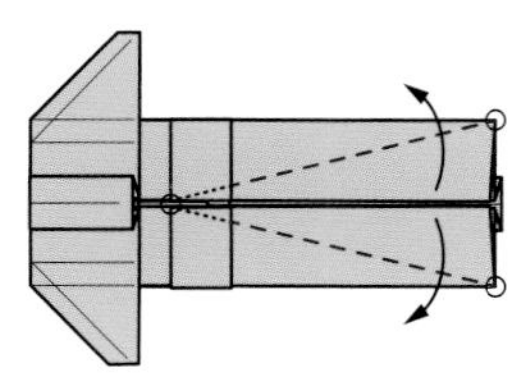

19 Fold the corners out between the points indicated.

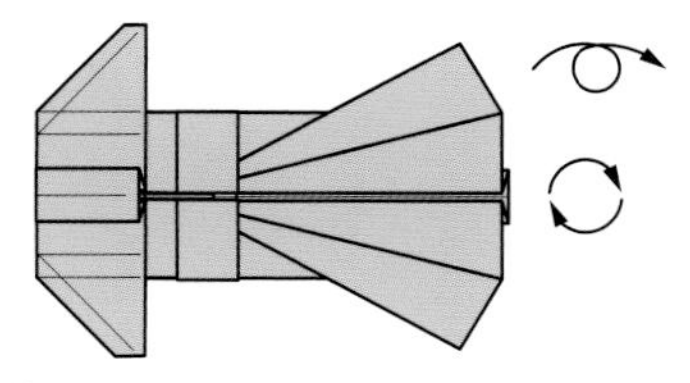

20 Rotate the model and turn it over.

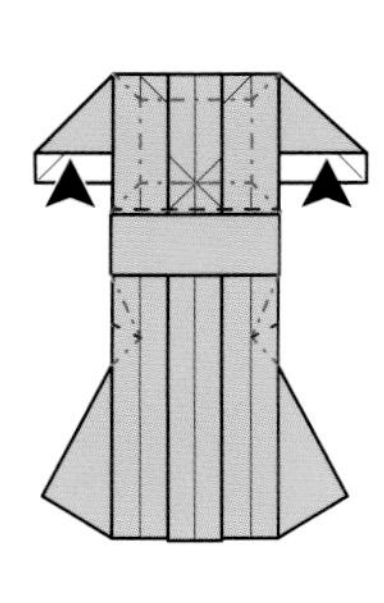

21 Open the sleeves to round them out and crease as indicated to make the dress three-dimensional.

The completed dress

MANTA RAY

1 Turn the paper over so the face side is down.

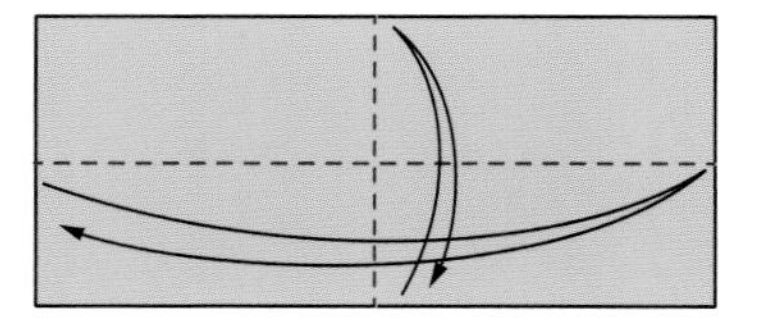

2 Fold in half horizontally and vertically. Unfold.

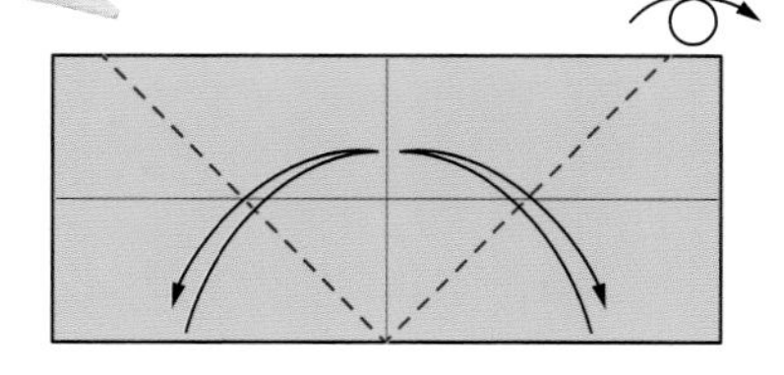

3 Fold the angle bisectors, edges to the crease line. Unfold. Turn over.

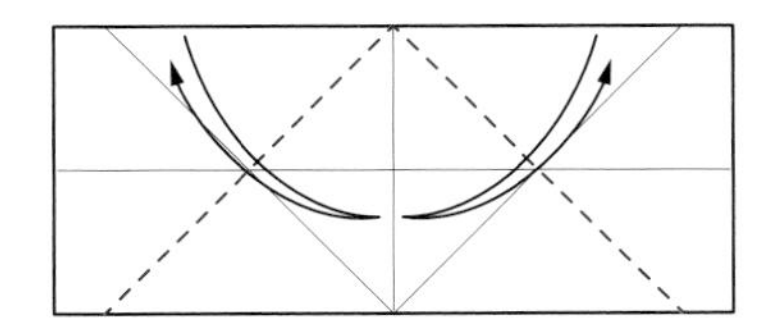

4 Fold the angle bisectors, edges to the crease line. Unfold.

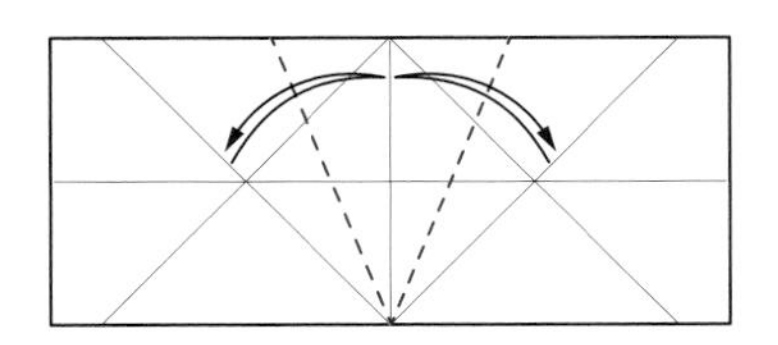

5 Fold the angle bisectors by folding the folded edges to the crease line. Unfold.

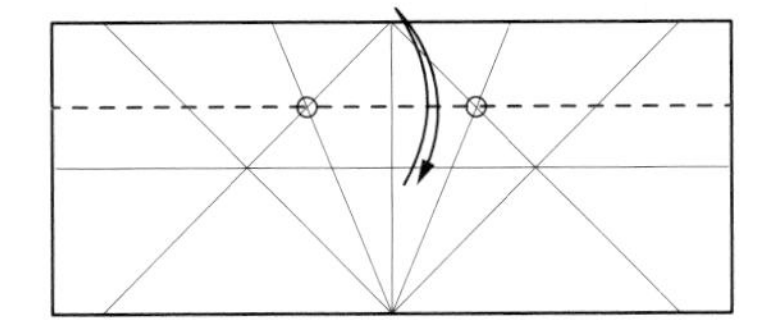

6 Fold horizontally through the references points indicated. Unfold.

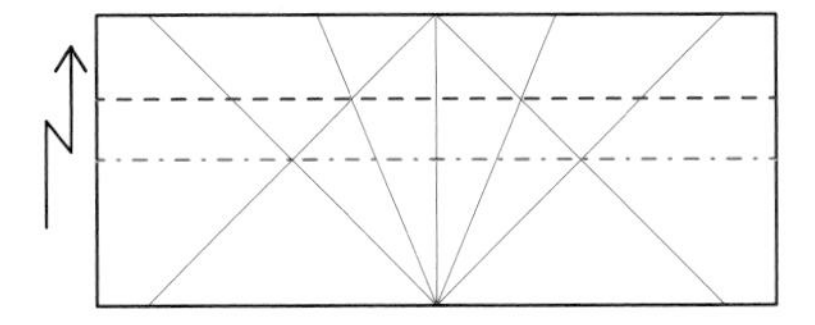

7 Pleat using existing creases.

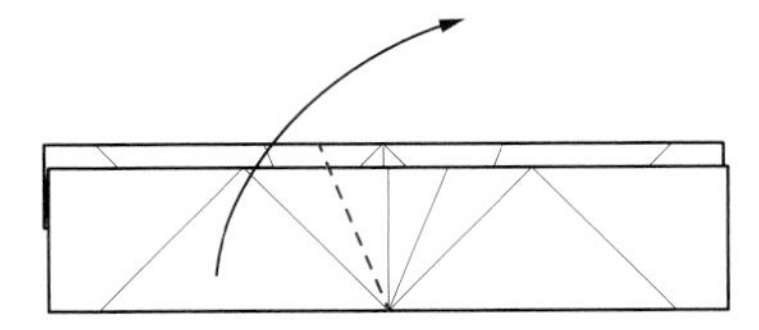

8 Valley fold through all layers, using the crease on the top layer as your guide.

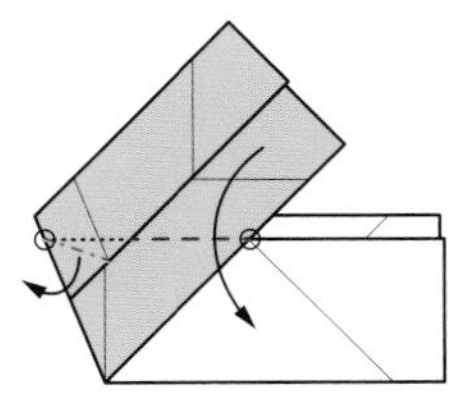

9 Make a new crease aligned to the folded edge beneath and then swivel the top layer to flatten.

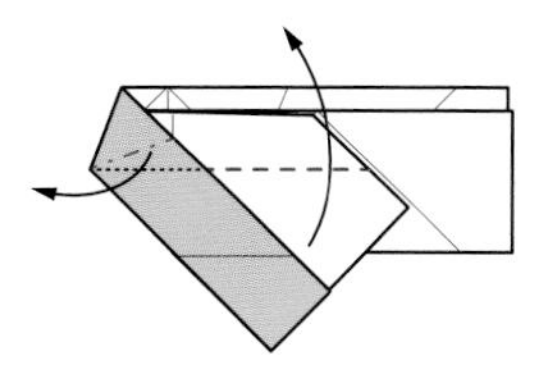

10 Valley fold up on the existing crease and swivel the corner to flatten.

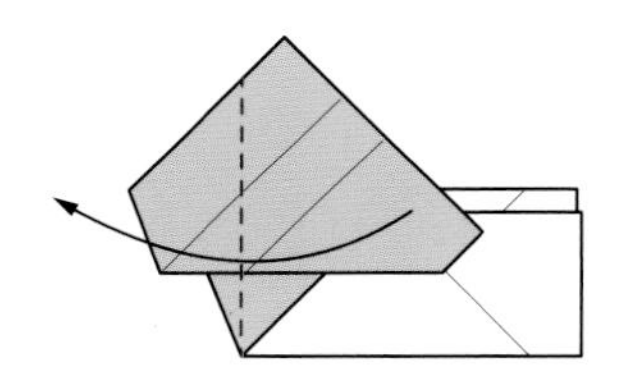

11 Valley fold the flap over on the existing crease.

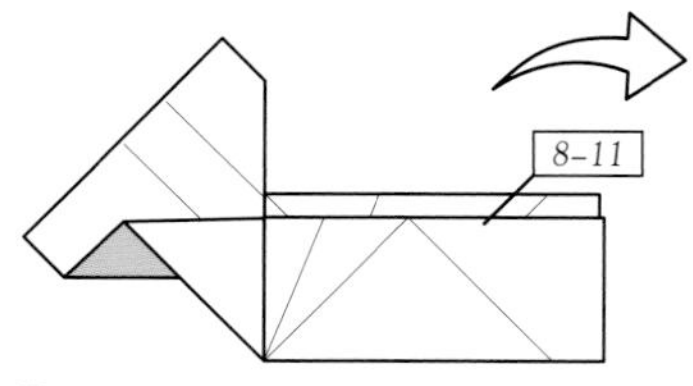

12 Repeat steps 8 to 11 on the other side.

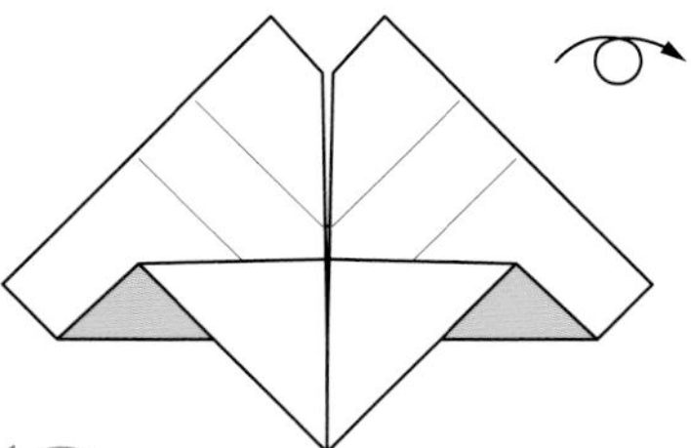

13 Turn over.

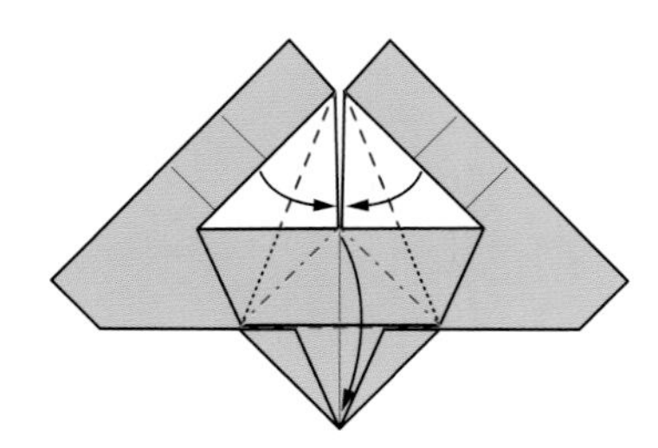

14 Petal fold.

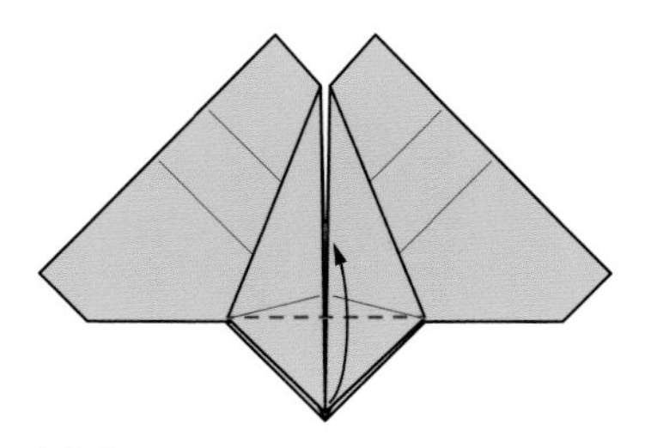

15 Valley fold the flap up.

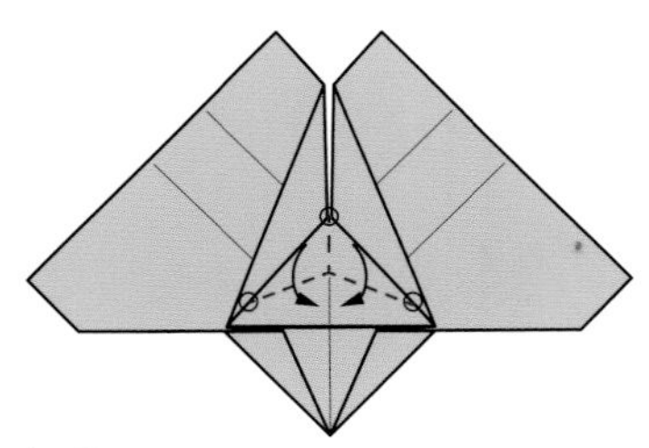

16 Rabbit-ear fold as shown, starting slightly above the corners, to create a fin. The fin will not lie flat.

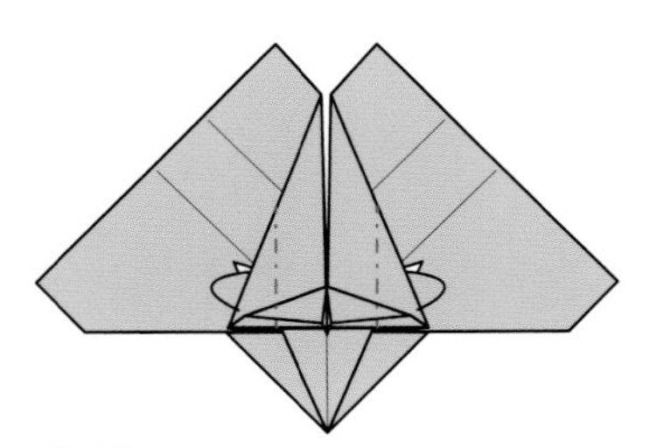

17 Mountain fold the corners in between the layers.

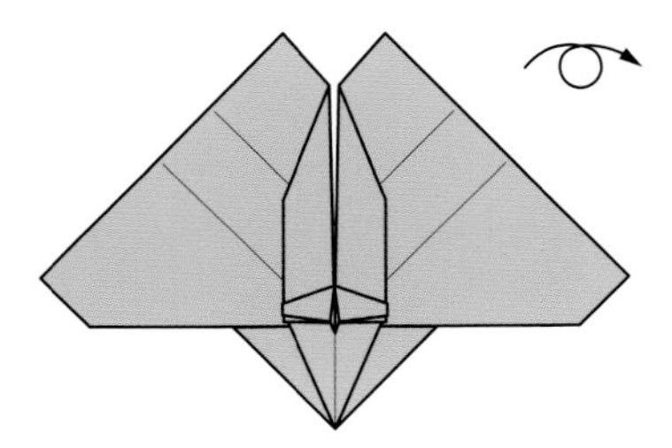

18 Turn over.

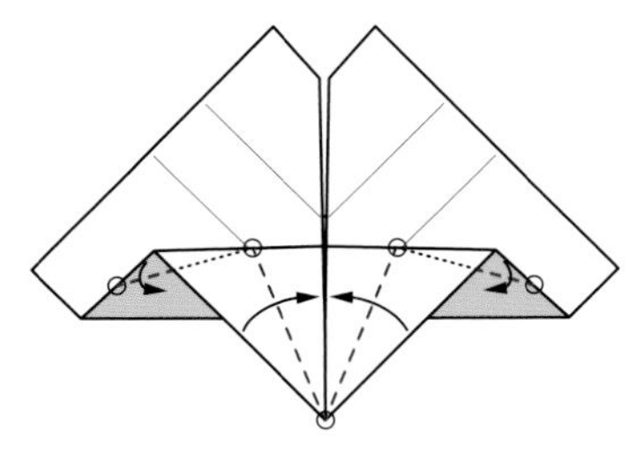

19 Swivel as indicated to narrow the corner (which will become the tail).

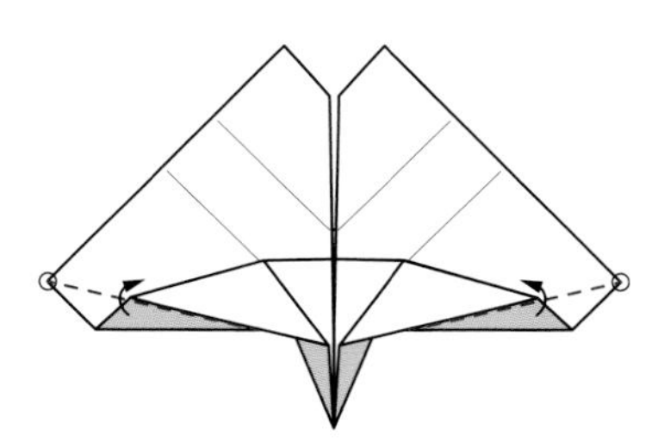

20 Valley fold the corners up.

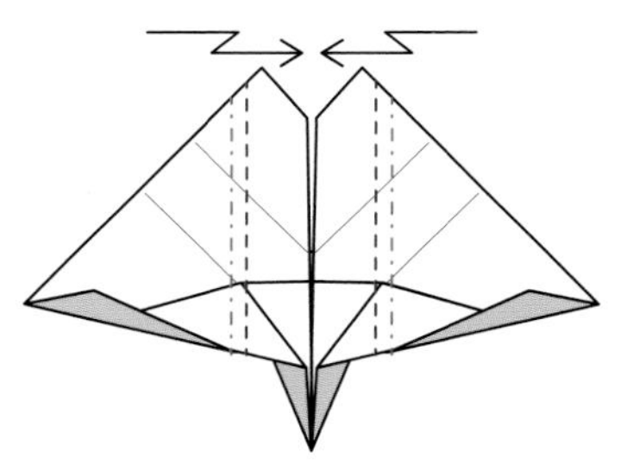

21 Pleat as indicated.

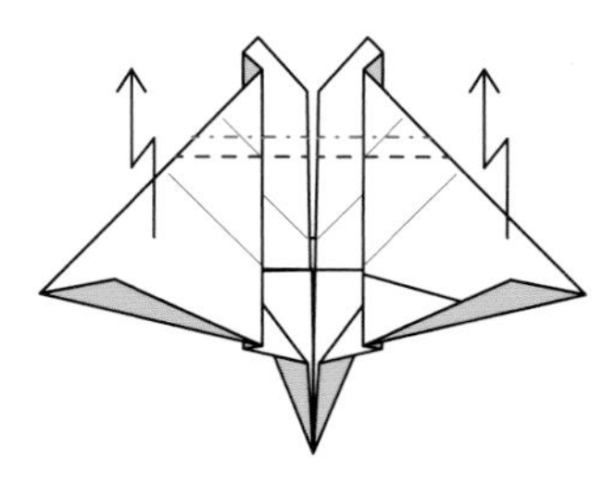

22 Pleat horizontally as indicated.

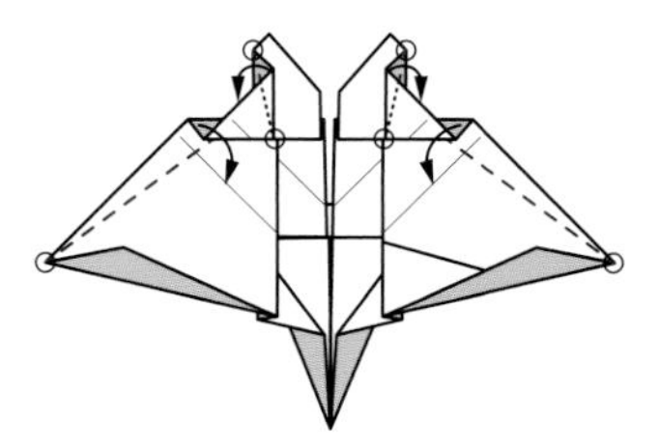

23 Open the pleat slightly and swivel the sides and corners as shown.

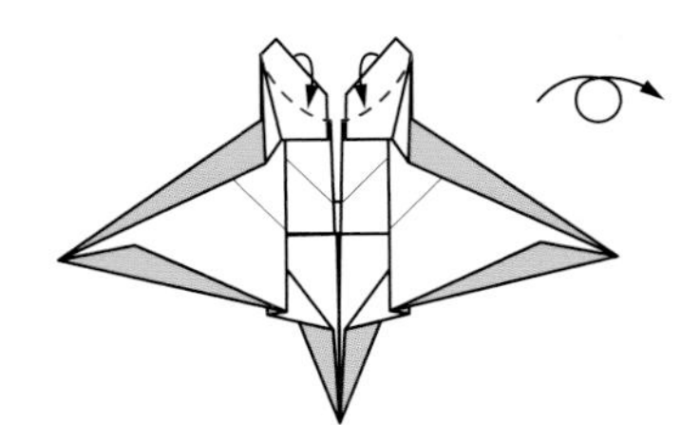

24 Valley fold as shown, making a curved three-dimensional crease, to form the cephalic lobes for the head. Turn over.

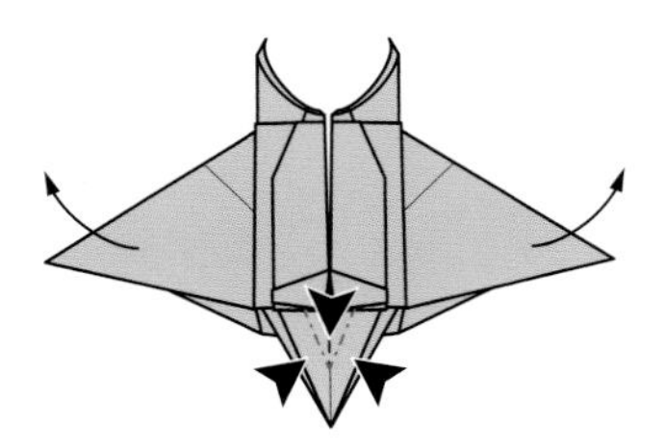

25 Shape the pectoral fins by giving them a little curl, then sink as shown to narrow the tail area.

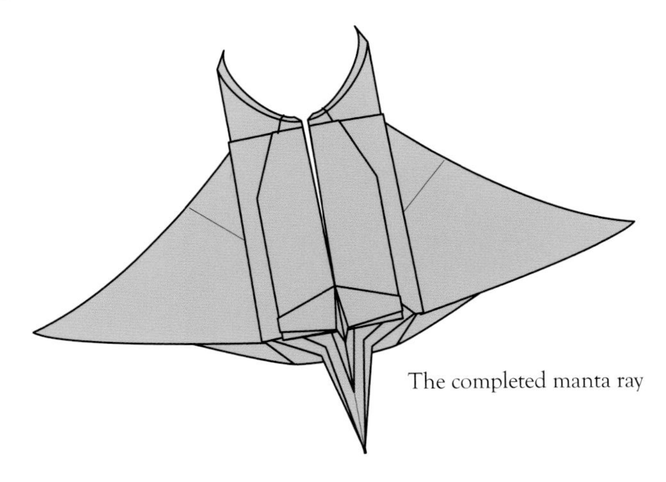

The completed manta ray

APPLE

You will need two bills for this model—one for the body of the fruit plus one for the stem and leaf.

Make the fruit first:

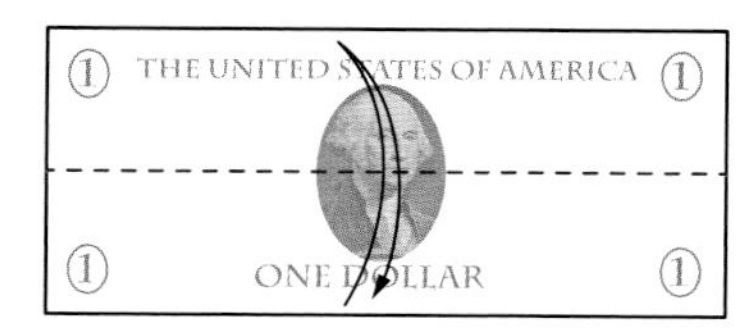

1 With the white (face) side up, fold in half. Unfold.

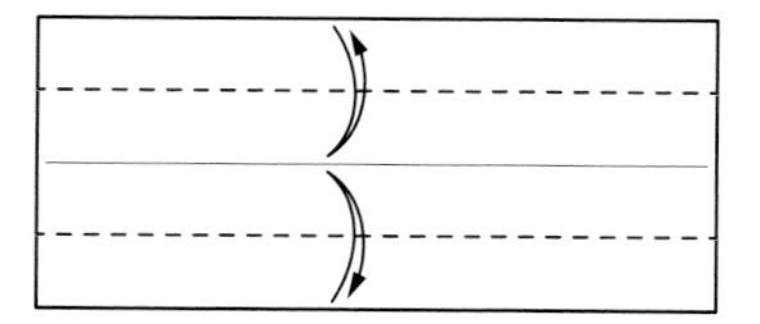

2 Fold in quarters. Unfold.

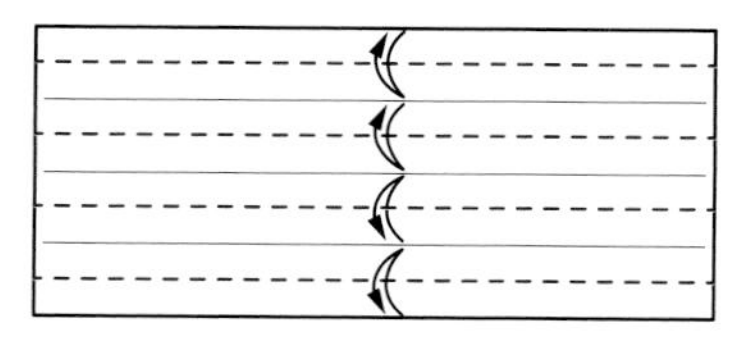

3 Fold in eighths. Unfold.

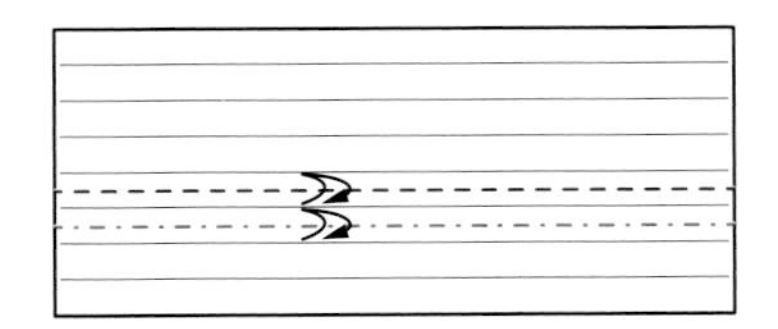

4 Crease between the creases as shown (note that one crease is valley and the other is mountain).

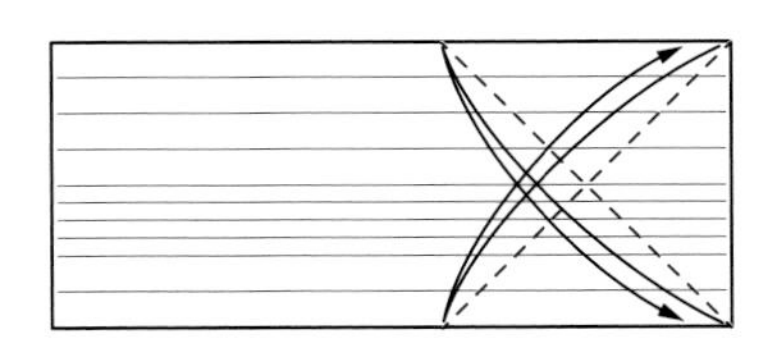

5 Fold the diagonals. Unfold.

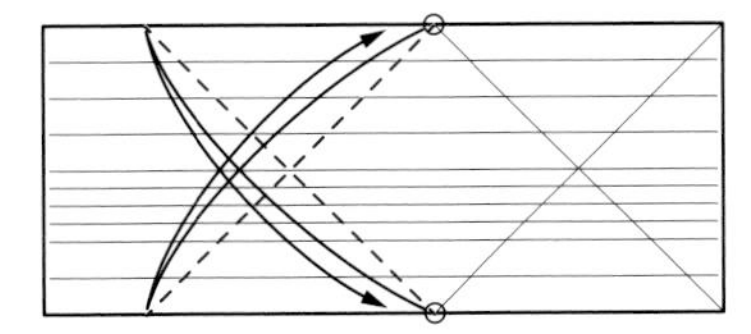

6 Fold the diagonals. Unfold.

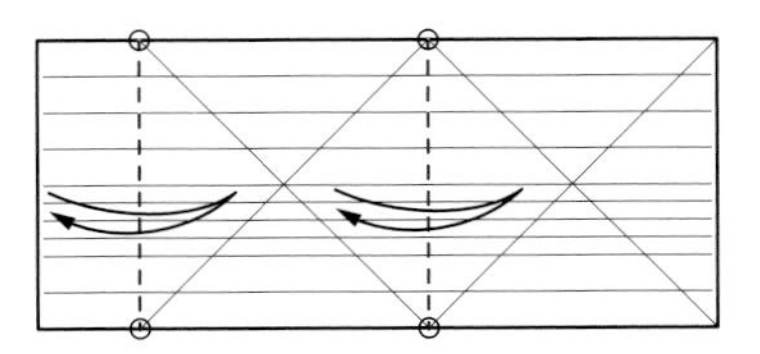

7 Crease between the reference points indicated.

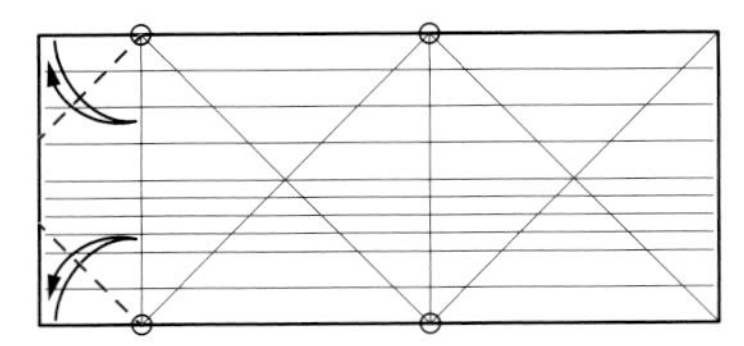

8 Fold the diagonals. Unfold.

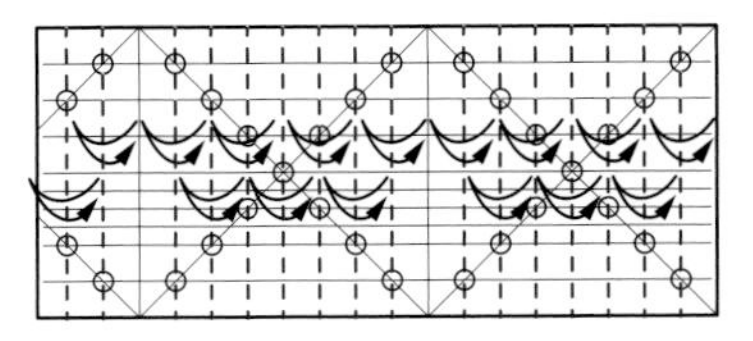

9 Crease between the intersection points indicated.

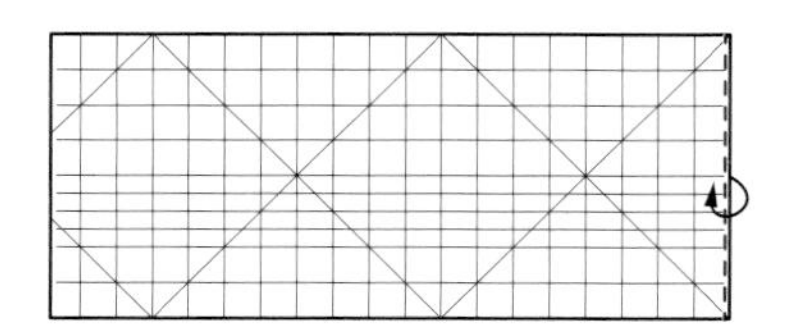

10 Fold a narrow flap at the edge.
It will help lock the model in place.

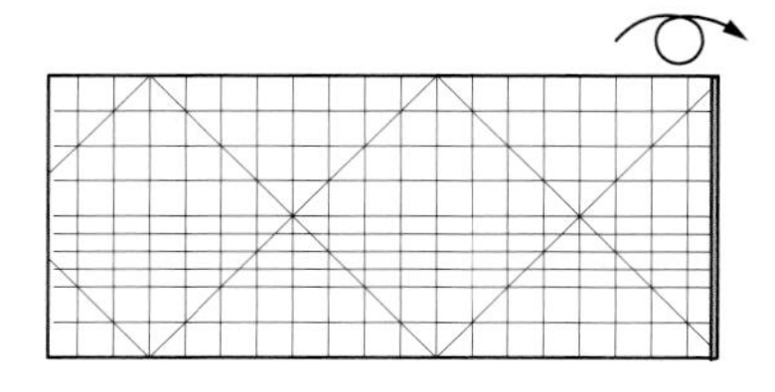

11 Turn over.

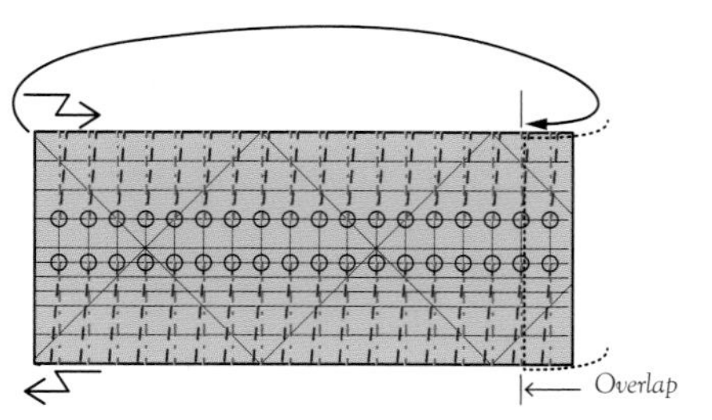

12 Create a sequence of pleats as shown to make the model three-dimensional, then roll it up into a cylinder, overlapping two pleats at the end.

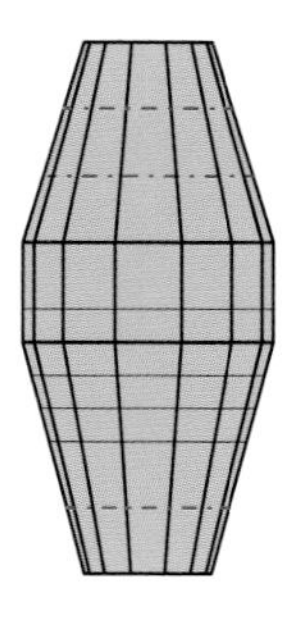

13 Mountain fold the top rows and the bottom to round out the model. See next step for expected result.

The finished fruit, folded and in cross section

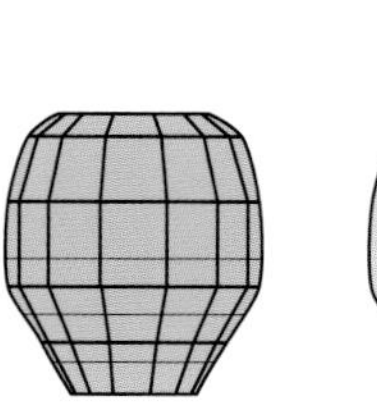

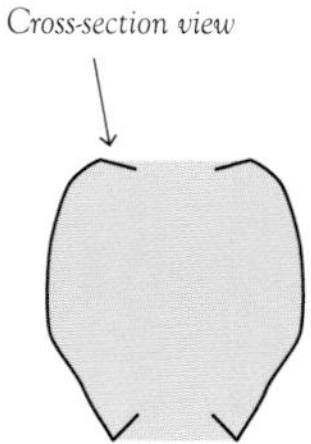

Make the stem and leaf:

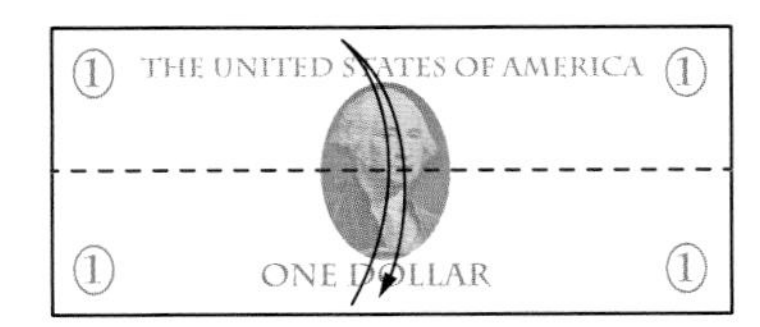

1 Fold in half. Unfold.

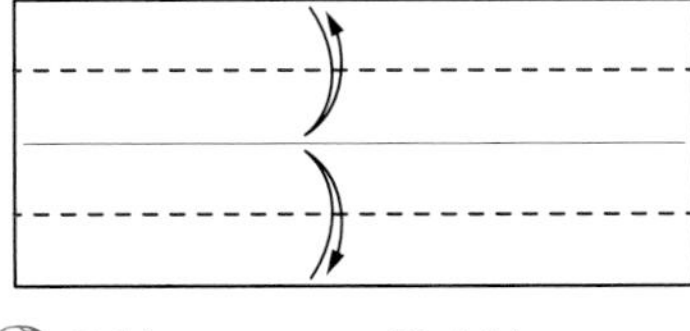

2 Fold in quarters. Unfold.

3 Fold the corners to the center crease.

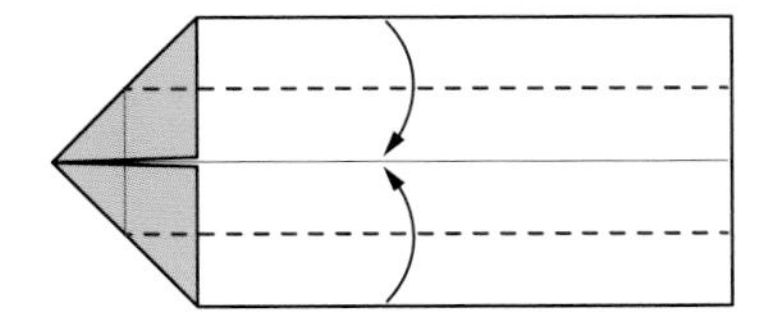

4 Fold the edges to the center crease.

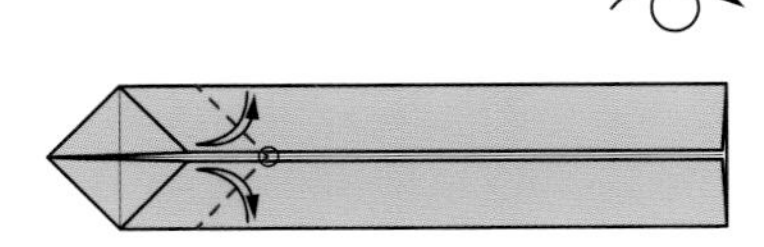

5 Valley fold the edges to the corners shown and unfold. Turn over.

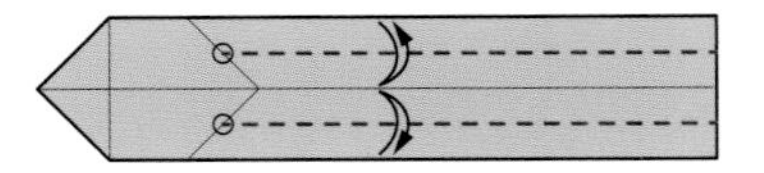

6 Fold the edges to the center, creasing as indicated. Unfold.

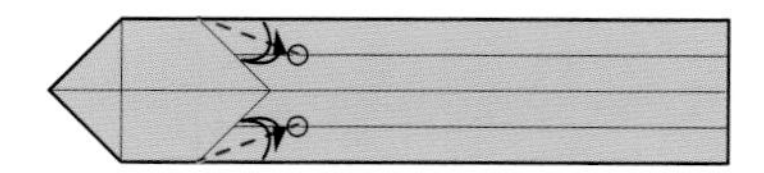

7 Fold the angle bisectors and unfold.

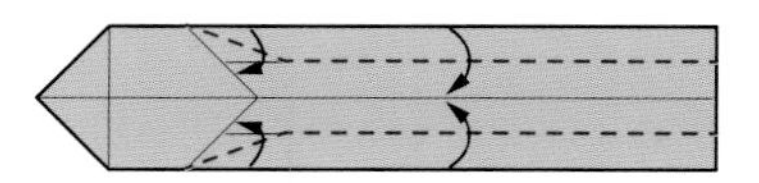

8 Valley fold on existing creases. Note: the model will not lie flat.

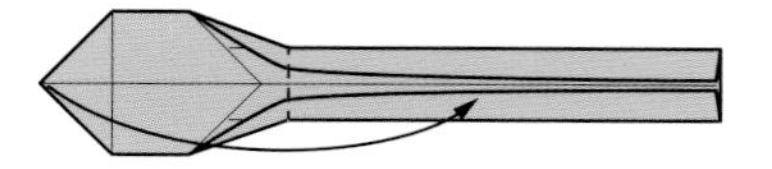

9 Valley fold and flatten.

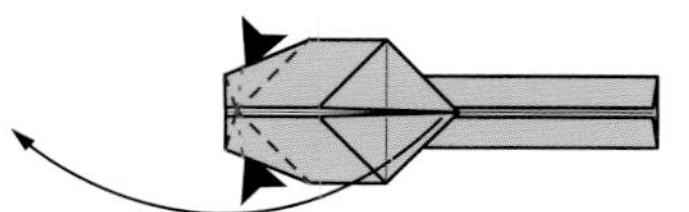

10 Start the swivel process with the valley folds, then mountain crease as shown. The model will not lie flat.

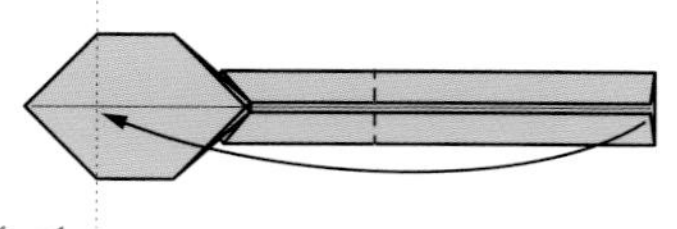

11 Valley fold.

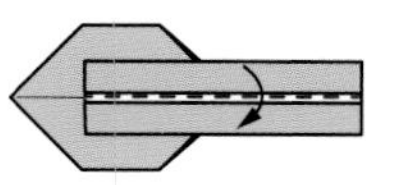

12 Keeping the leaf flat, valley fold the stem edge to the bottom.

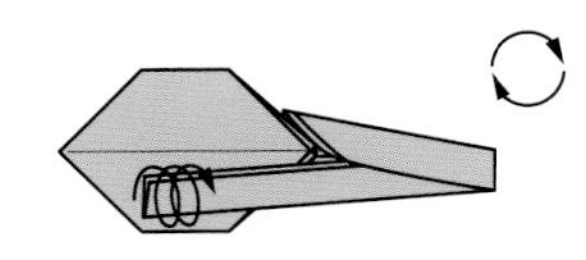

13 Twist to round the stem. Rotate.

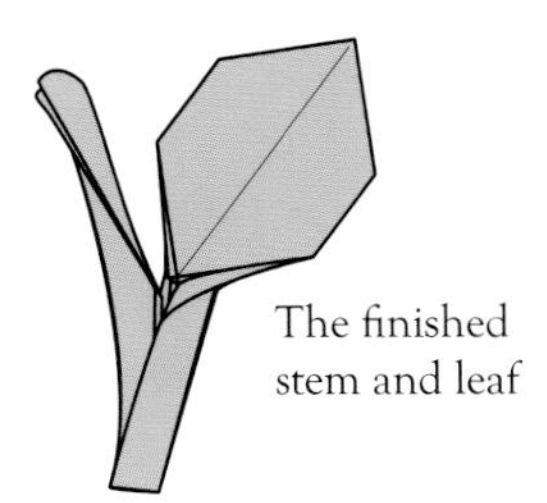

The finished stem and leaf

Assemble the sections:

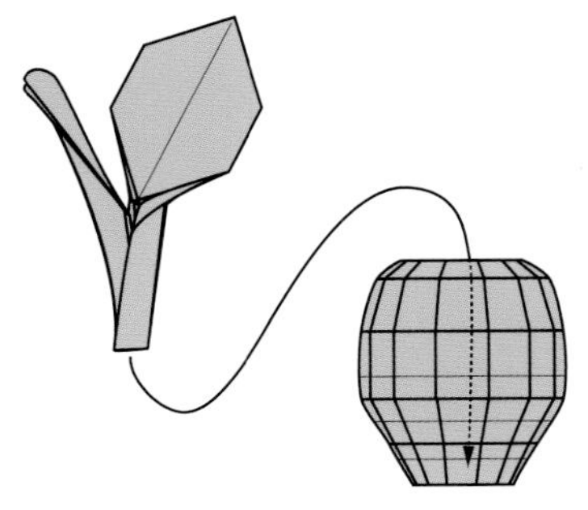

Insert the stem into the body of the fruit.

The completed apple

JACKET

You will need two bills to make this model.

Make the sleeves first:

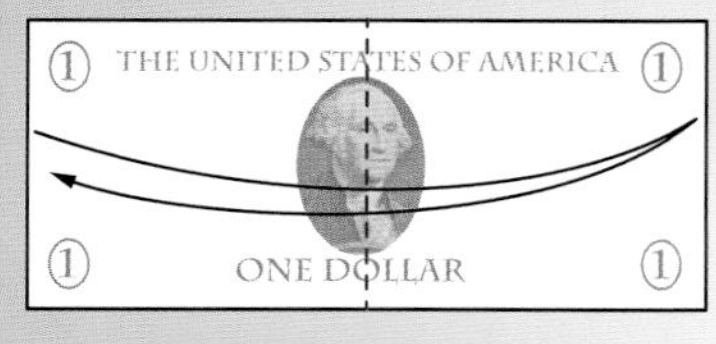

1 With the first bill positioned white (face) side up, fold in half vertically and unfold.

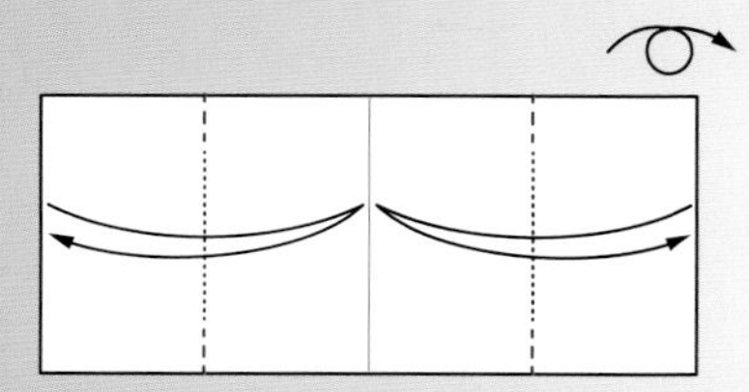

2 Fold the edges to the center crease, but crease at the edges only. Turn over.

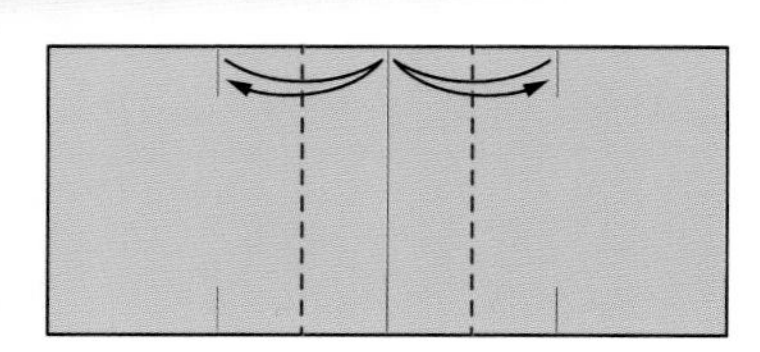

3 Fold the pinch marks to the center crease. Unfold.

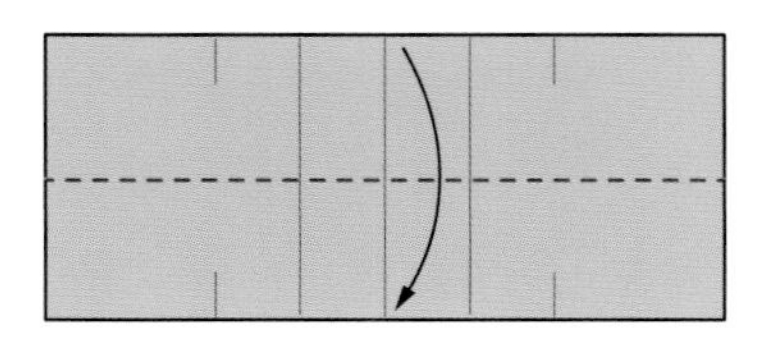

4 Fold the top edge to the bottom edge. Turn over.

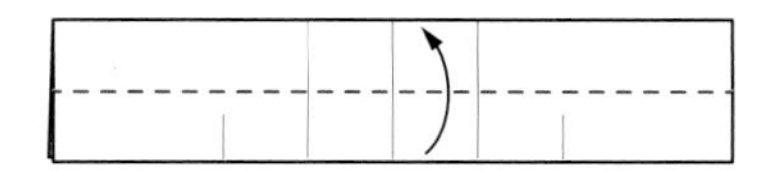

5 Fold the edge to the folded edge.

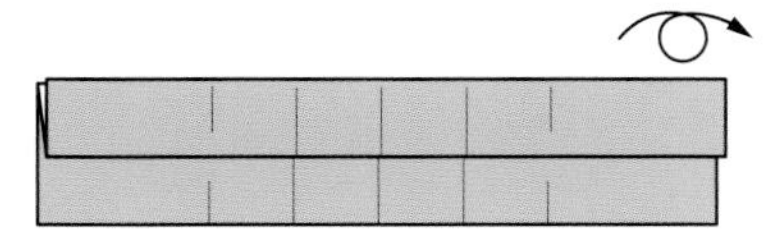

6 Turn over.

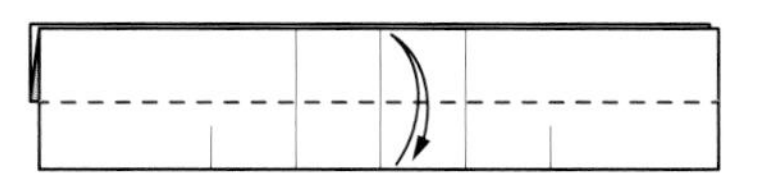

7 Fold the edge to the folded edge. Unfold. Note: the next steps may be folded simultaneously on the left and right, since they will be repeated.

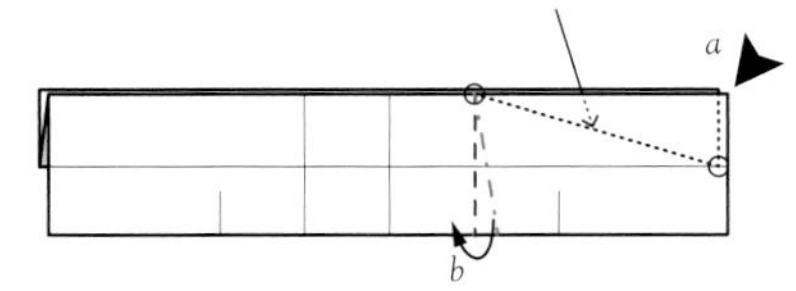

8 Mountain fold on the middle layer as indicated (see *a* in diagram). Then swivel by valley folding on the existing crease and forming a new mountain crease (see *b* in diagram).

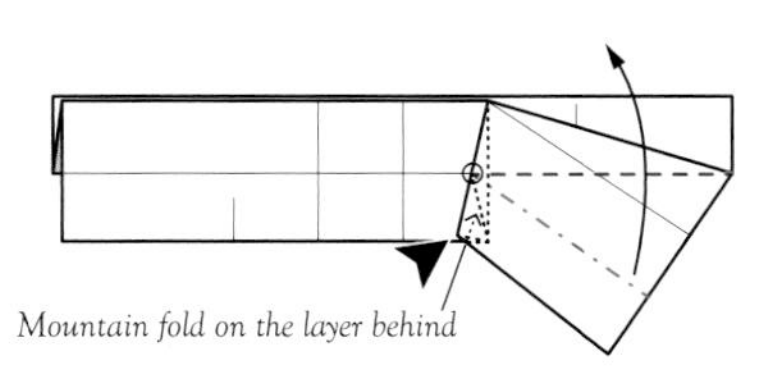

9 Swivel on the top layer as indicated. A small new mountain crease will be needed on the middle layer to make the model lie flat. See next step for the result.

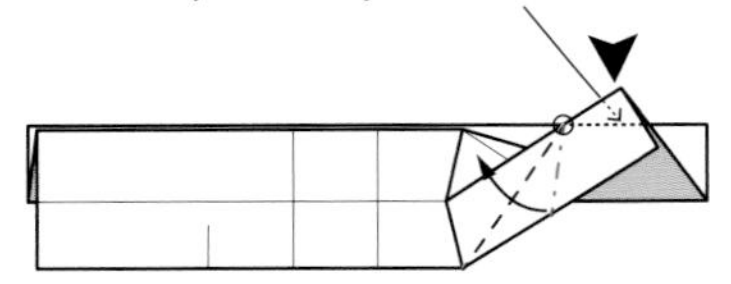

10 Mountain fold on the middle layer as indicated (parallel to the folded edge), then swivel as indicated. See the next step for the result.

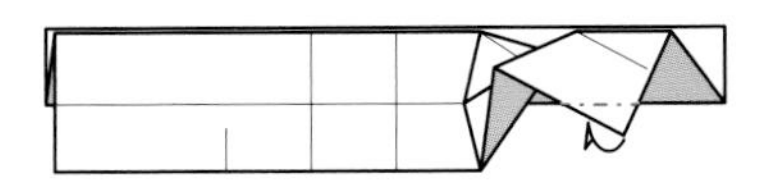

11 Mountain fold along the edge.

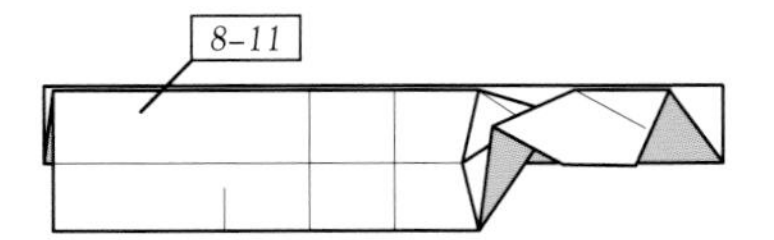

12 If you haven't already repeated steps 8 to 11 on the other side, do that now.

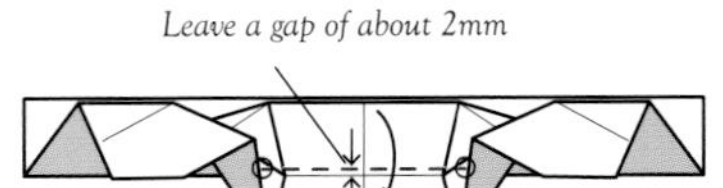

13 Valley fold as indicated, leaving a small gap (about 2mm) between the new crease and the existing one. The model will not lie flat.

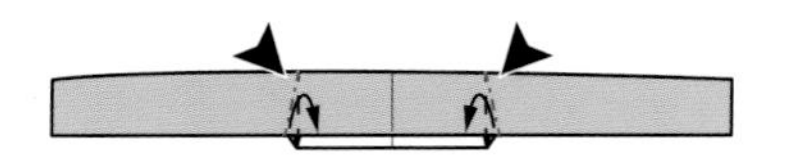

14 Crimp and squash to flatten.

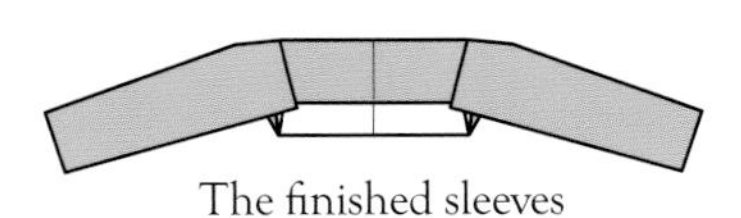

The finished sleeves

Use another bill to fold the body of the jacket:

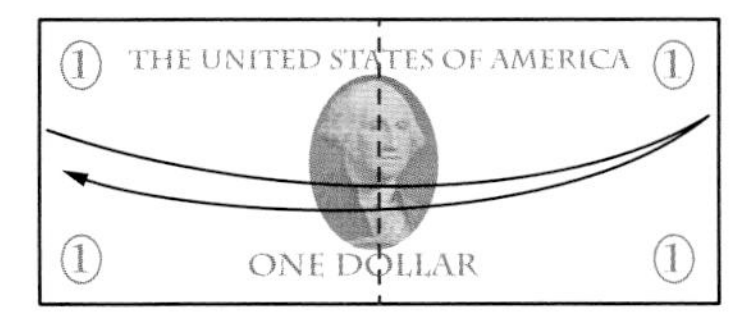

1 With the white (face) side up, fold the bill in half vertically. Unfold.

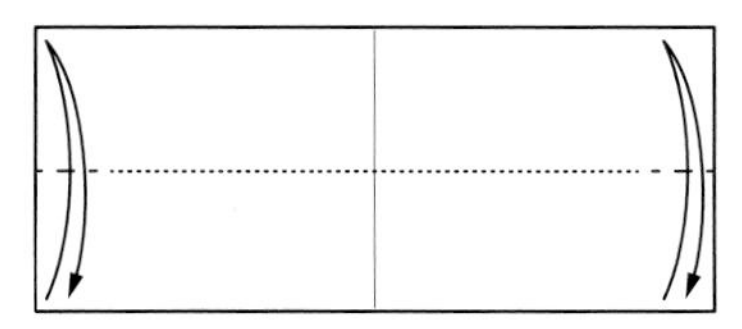

2 Fold the bottom edge to the top, creasing only at the sides. Unfold.

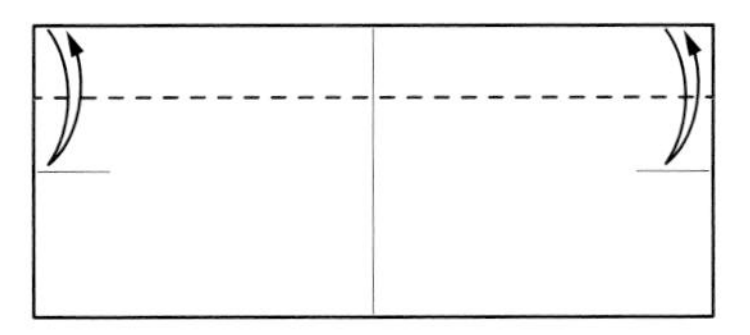

3 Fold the top edge to the pinch marks. Unfold.

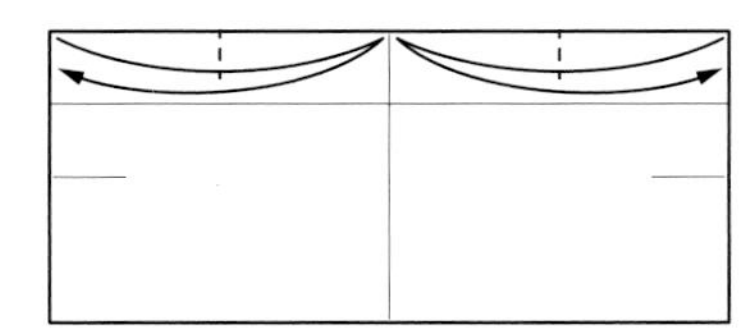

4 Fold the side edges to the center crease, pinching at the top edge only.

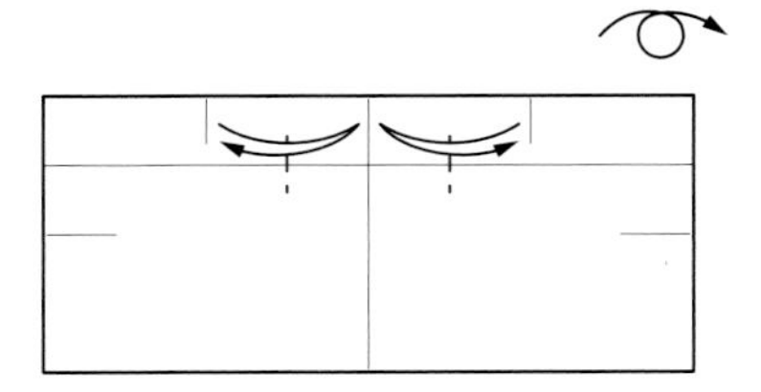

5 Fold the pinch marks made in step 4 to the center crease, creasing each only where it crosses the horizontal crease formed in step 3. Turn over.

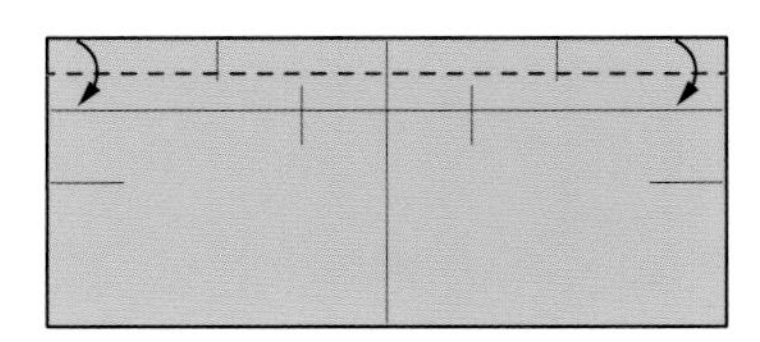

6 Fold the top edge to the crease indicated.

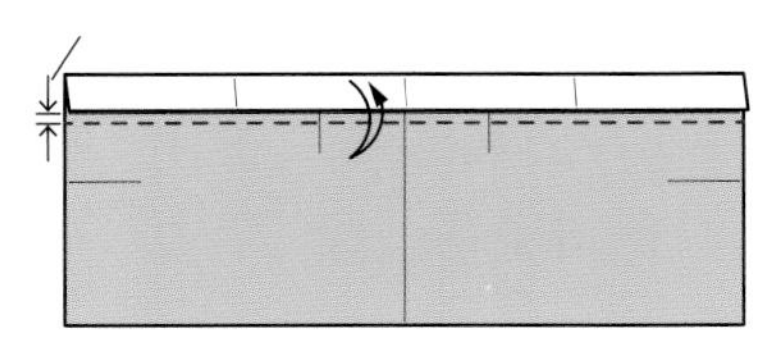

7 Valley fold about 1mm below the crease line. Unfold.

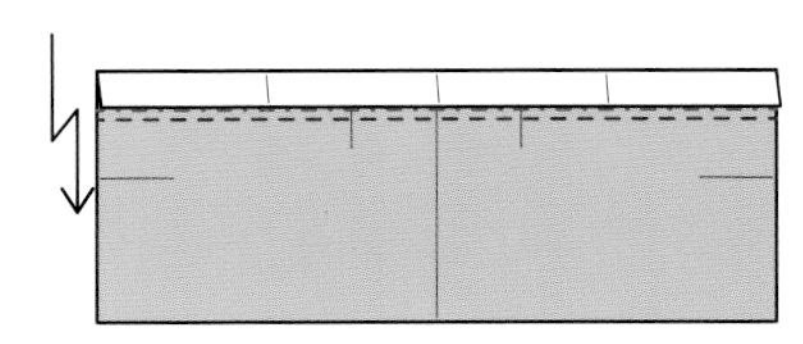

8 Pleat using the creases formed in steps 6 and 7.

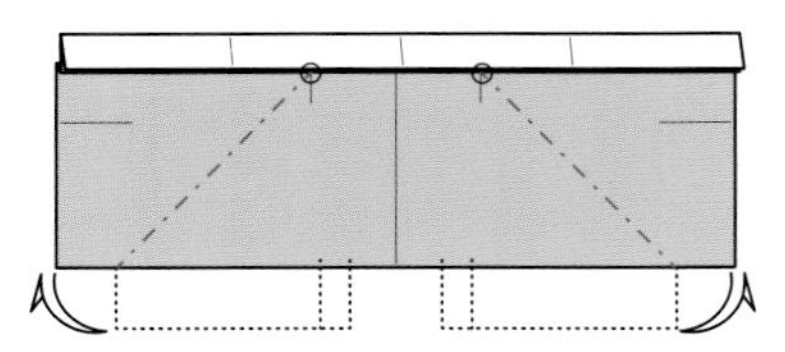

9 Mountain fold the diagonals shown so the side edges are parallel with the center crease. Start the folds at the reference points shown, but they can also be started 1mm closer to the center crease because the layers are thick. Unfold.

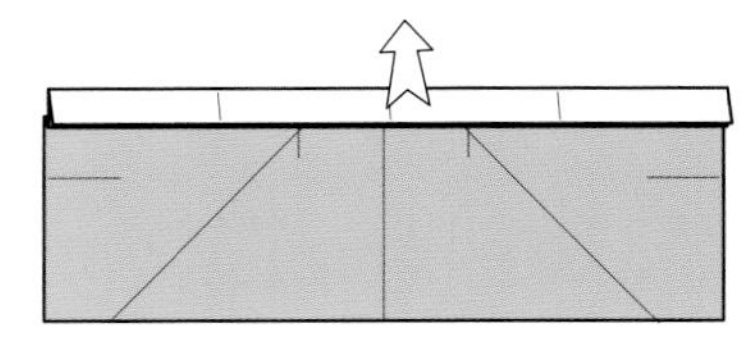

10 Unfold the pleat created in step 8.

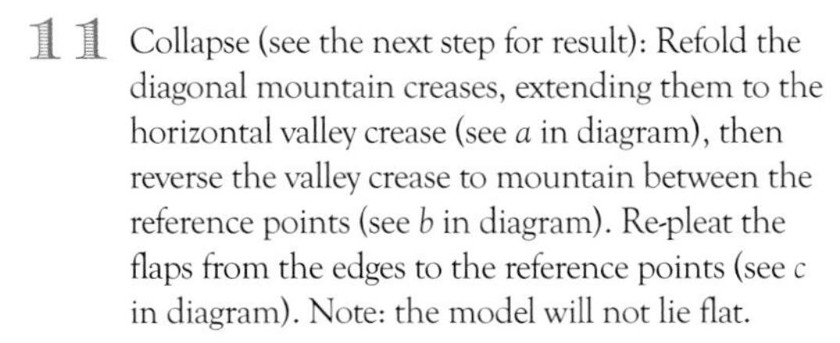

11 Collapse (see the next step for result): Refold the diagonal mountain creases, extending them to the horizontal valley crease (see *a* in diagram), then reverse the valley crease to mountain between the reference points (see *b* in diagram). Re-pleat the flaps from the edges to the reference points (see *c* in diagram). Note: the model will not lie flat.

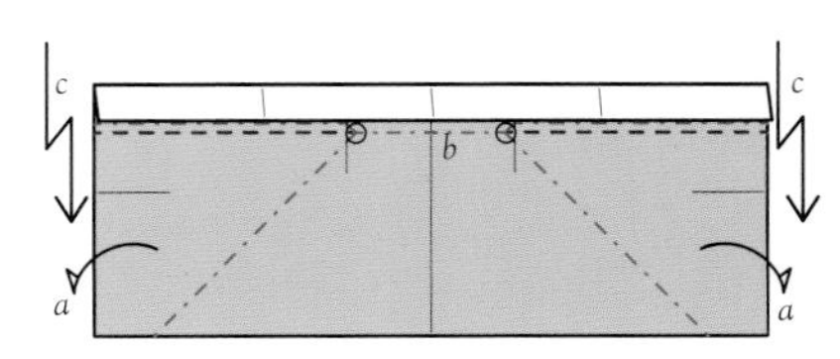

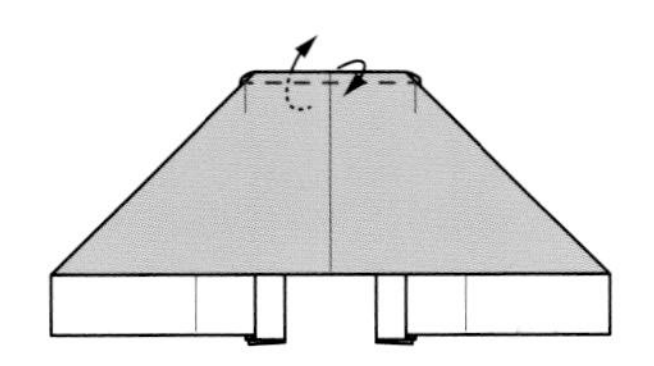

12 Valley fold the long narrow flap, allowing the paper from behind to flip out. The model will still not lie flat.

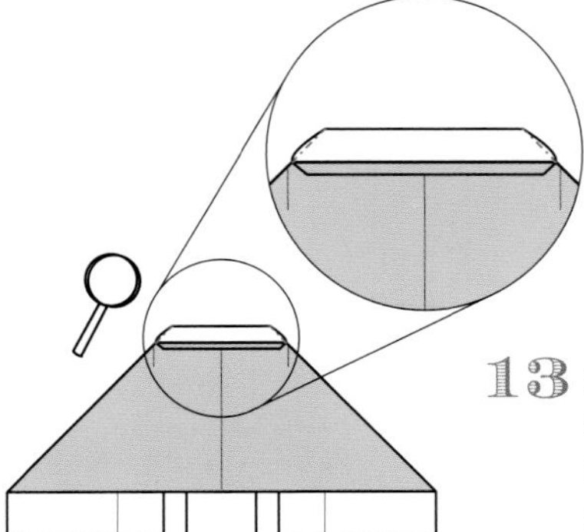

13 Mountain crease the edges shown to make the model lie flat.

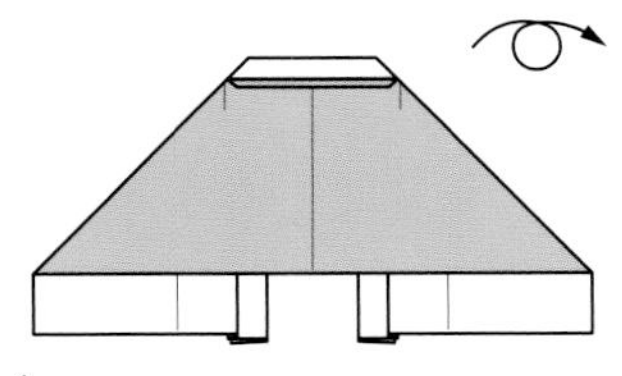

14 Turn over.

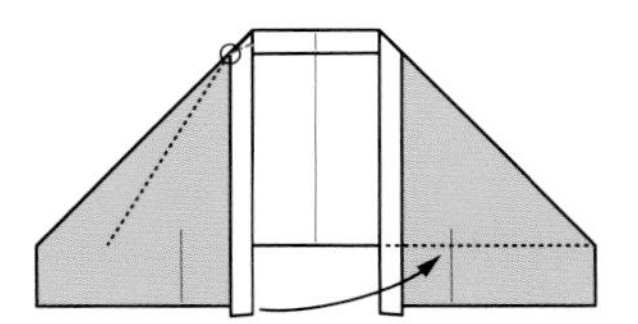

15 Pivoting from the reference point, swivel the paper as indicated, keeping it flat. See the next step for the result.

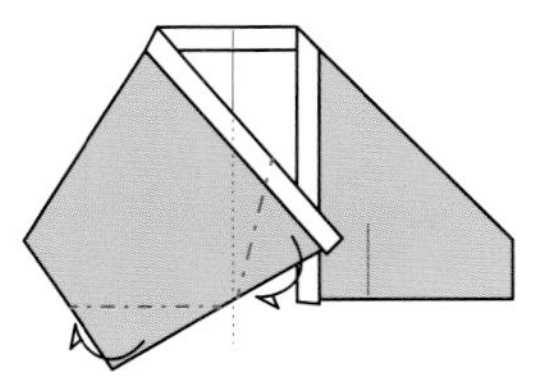

16 Mountain fold as indicated.

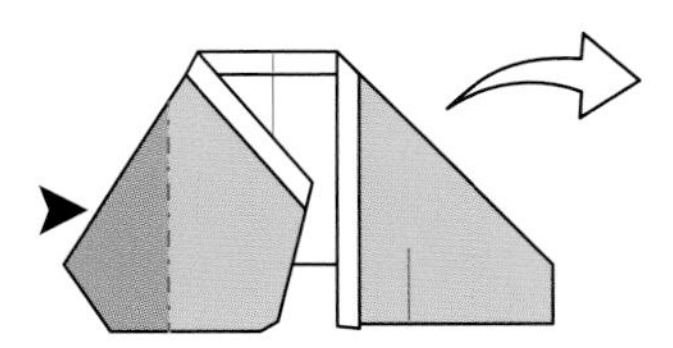

17 Reverse fold as indicated.

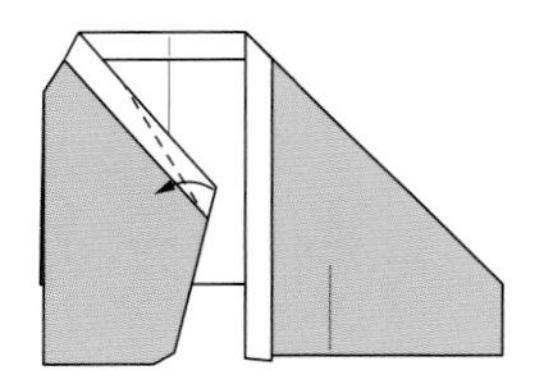

18 Form the lapels: Valley fold as indicated.

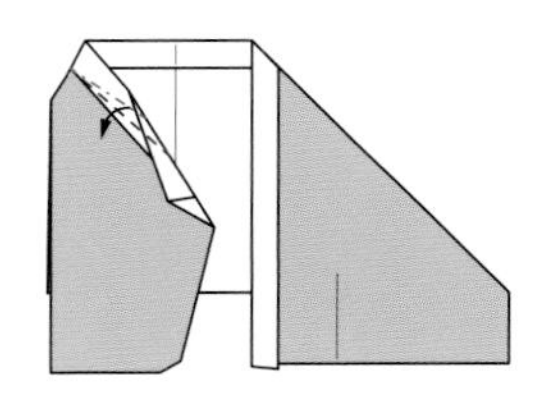

19 Swivel.

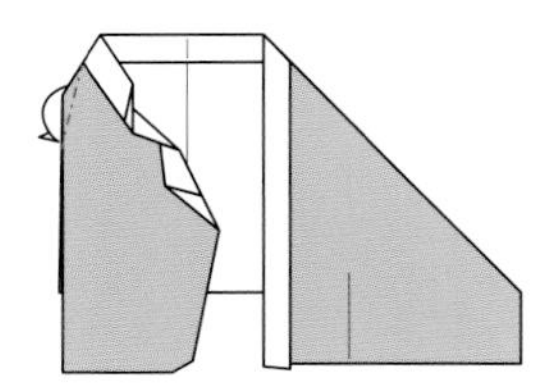

20 Mountain fold the corner to shape the shoulder.

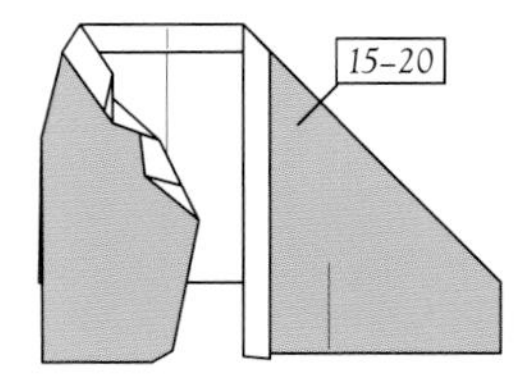

21 Repeat steps 15 through 20 on the other side.

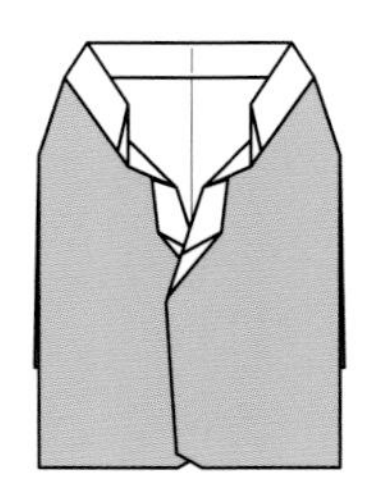

The finished body of the jacket

Assemble the pieces:

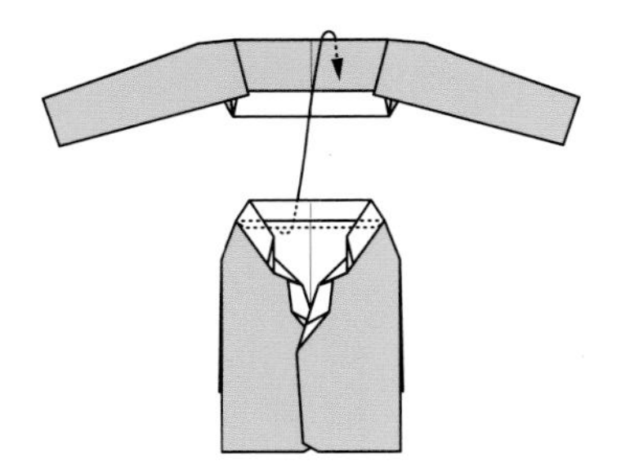

1 Position the sleeves under the body, just under the narrow pleat that is below the collar.

2 Bring the corners of the sleeves to the front to lock the units together.

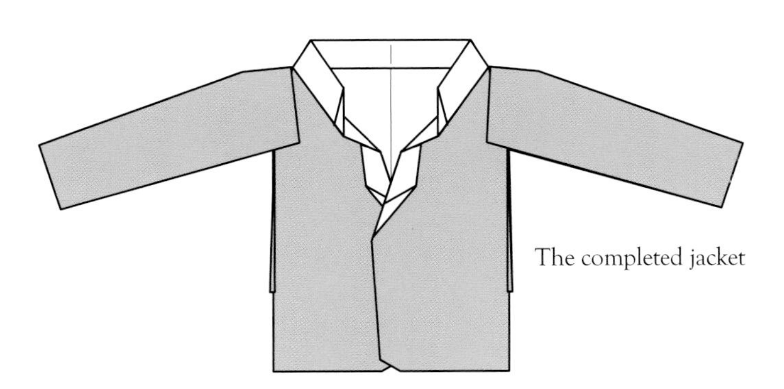

The completed jacket

OWL

This model cannot be made with the practice currency in this kit because facial details require elements that appear on the back of a real dollar bill.

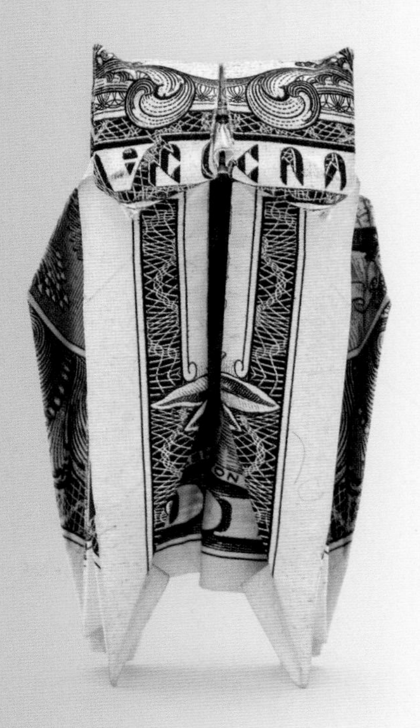

1 Select a bill with printing that is perfectly centered. Place the back (green ink) face up and valley fold in half. Unfold.

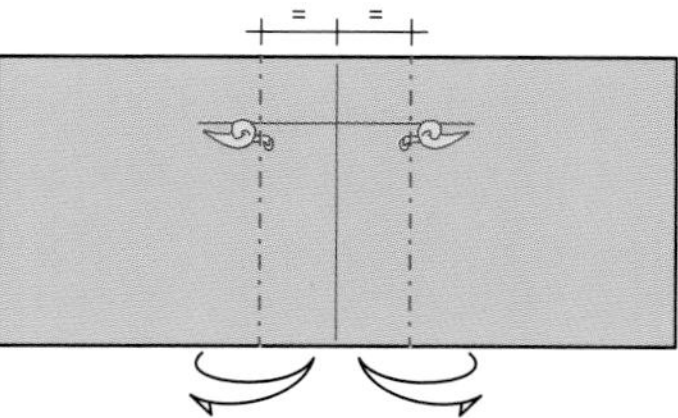

2 Notice the decorative swirls above "In God We Trust." Make mountain creases as shown next to the swirls.

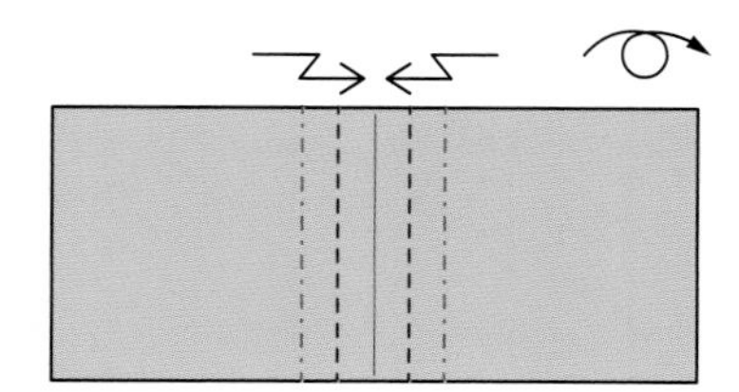

3 Pleat. Turn over.

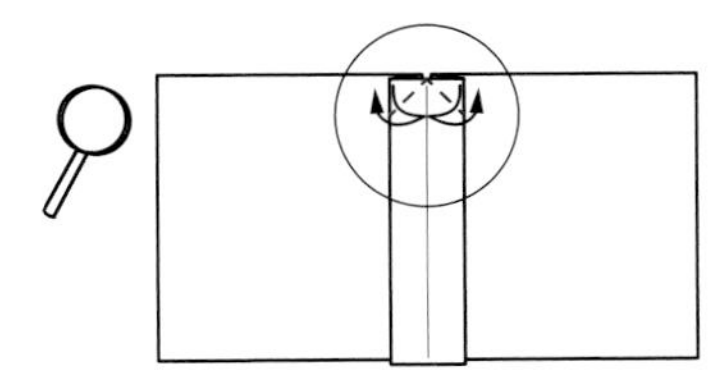

4 Fold the angle bisectors and unfold.

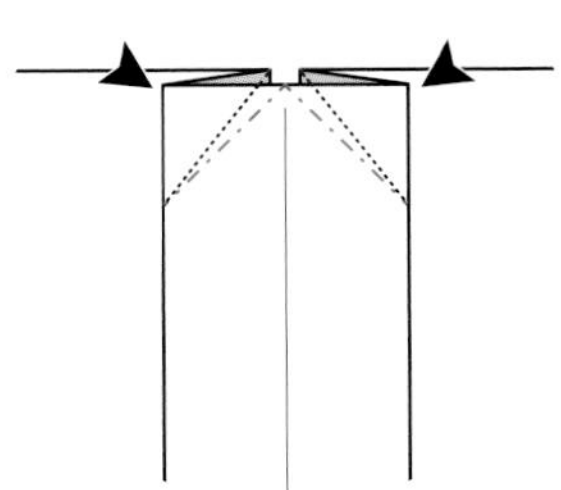

5 Reverse fold the corners.

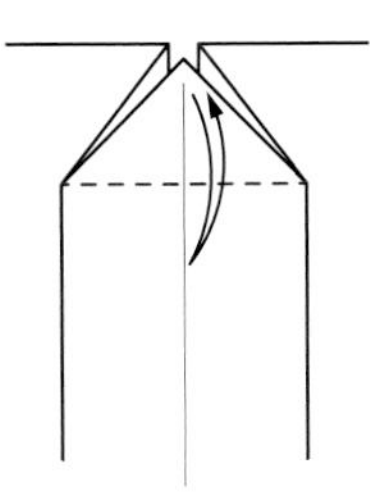

6 Fold the new corner down and unfold, making a new crease from corner to corner.

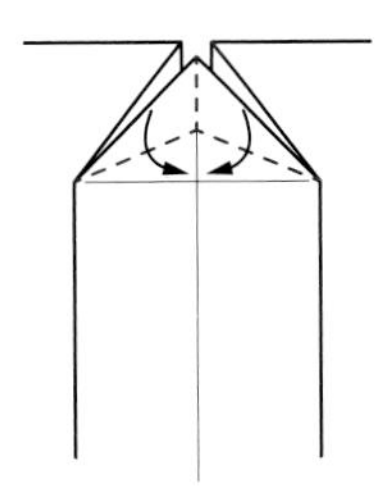

7 Rabbit-ear the triangular flap. This will create a point that will not lie flat.

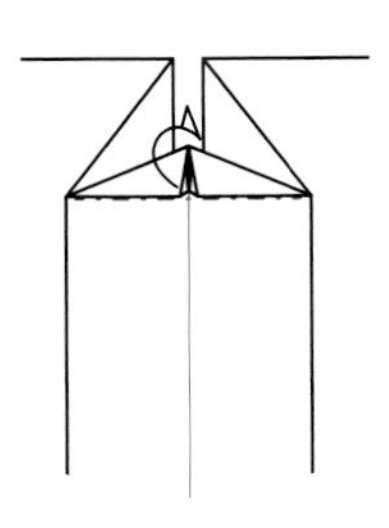

8 Fold the completed rabbit ear inside. The point will stick out between the folded edges, making the owl's beak.

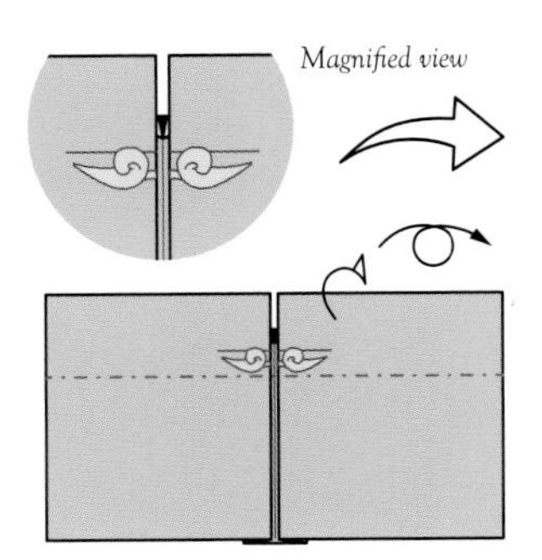

9 Mountain fold as shown, just below the swirls. Turn over.

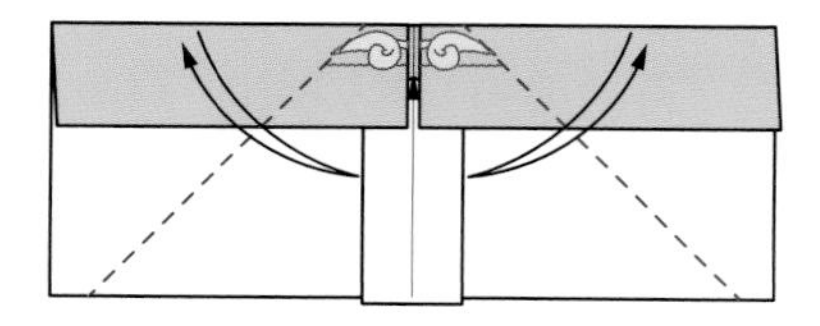

10 Fold the angle bisectors. Unfold.

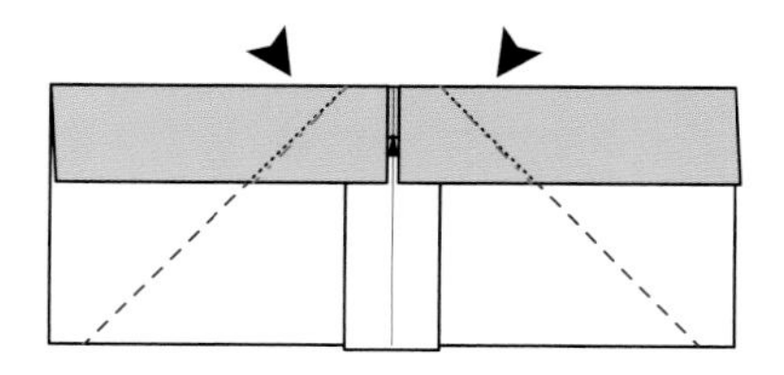

11 Reverse fold both sides as indicated.

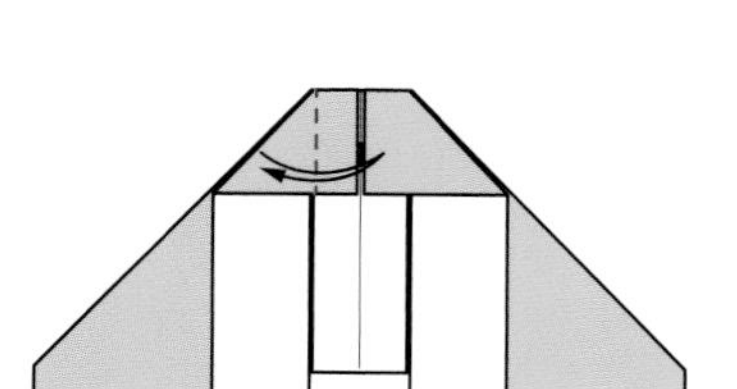

12 Fold and unfold to make the vertical crease.

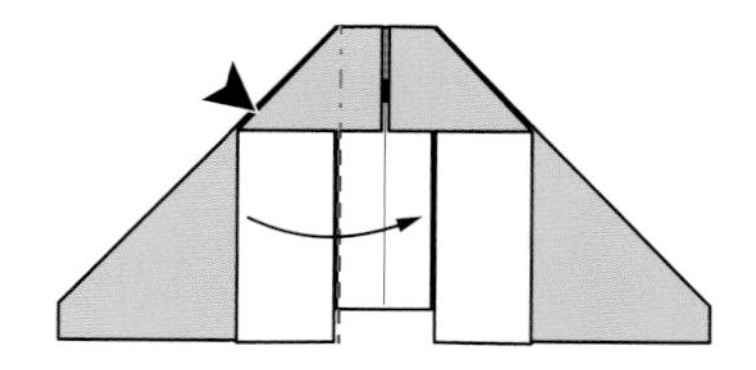

13 Reverse fold the corner.

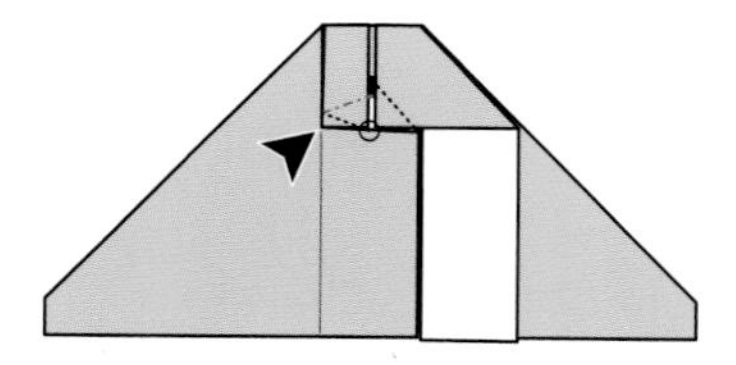

14 Reverse fold as shown.

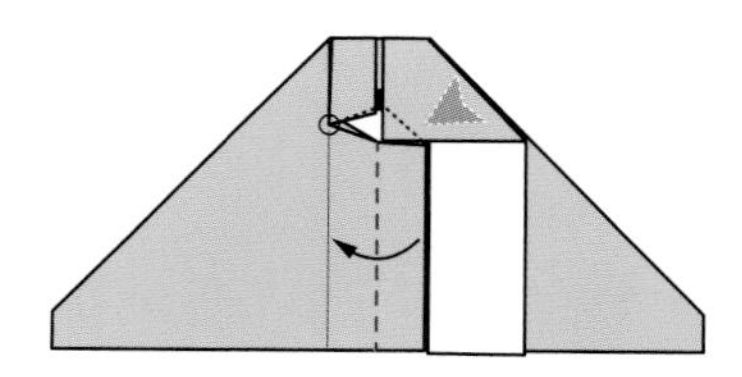

15 Reverse fold the flap at the hidden corner.

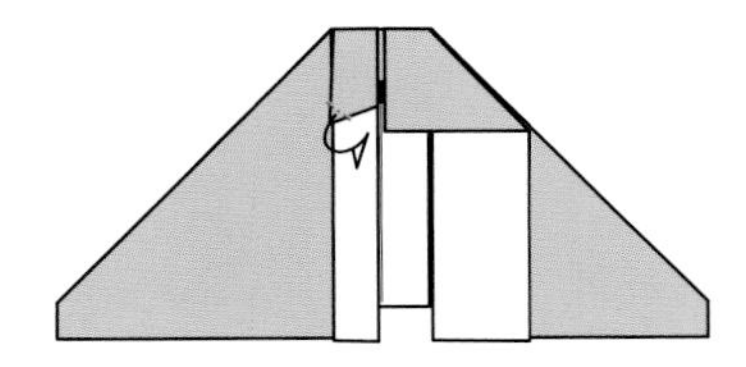

16 Fold the corner behind.

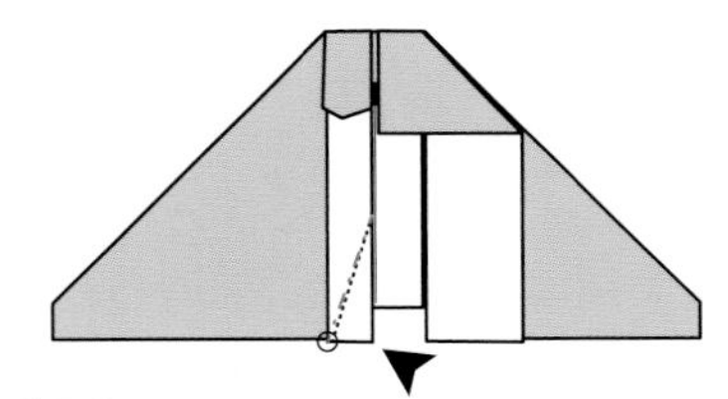

17 Mountain fold the corner and then reverse fold as shown.

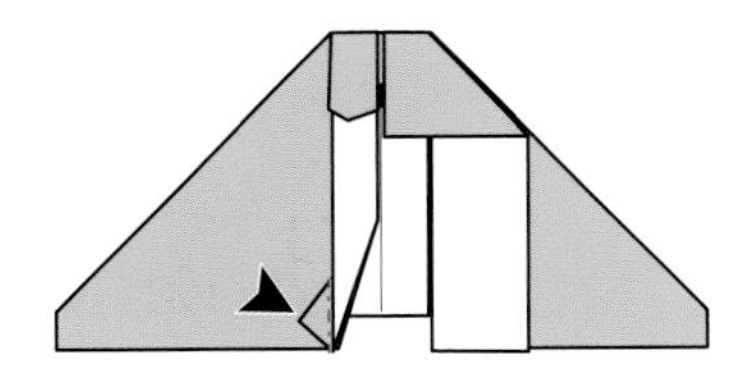

18 Fold along the folded edge and then reverse fold the corner.

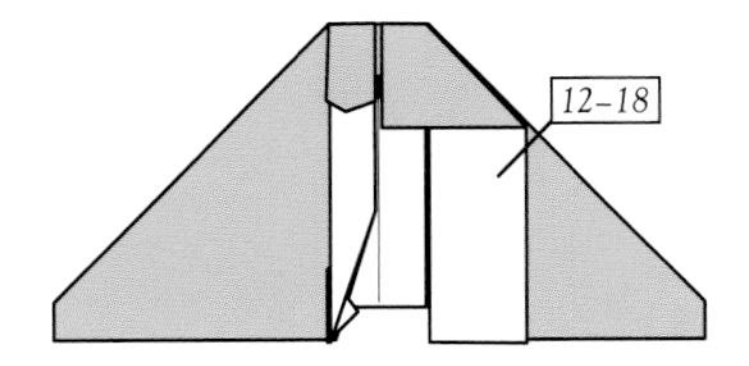

19 Repeat steps 12 to 18 on the other side.

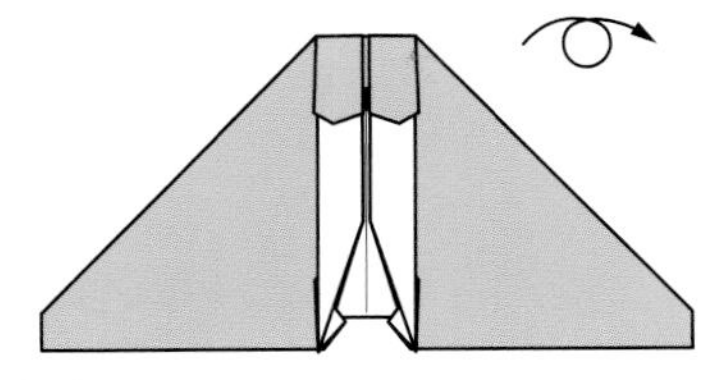

20 Turn the model over.

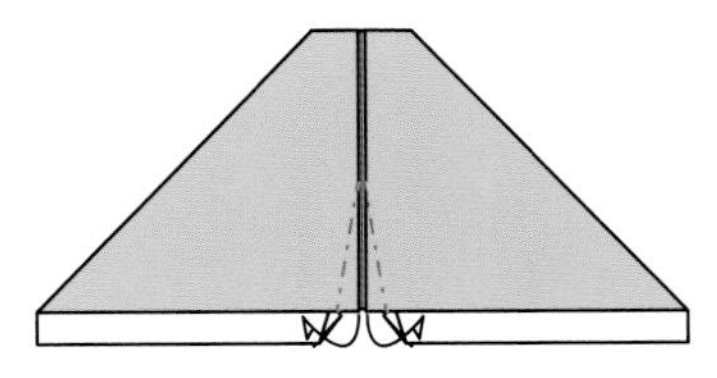

21 Mountain fold the corners behind as indicated.

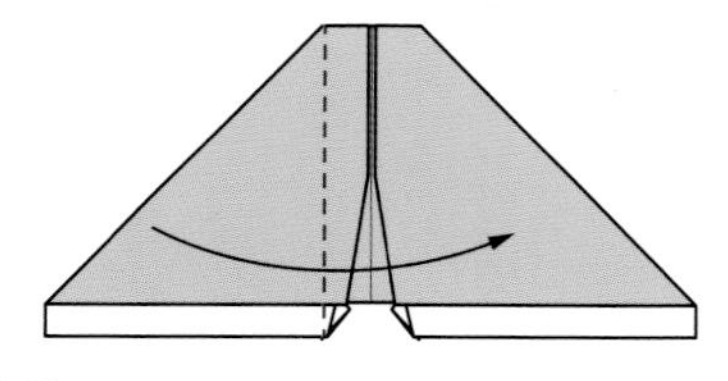

22 Valley fold the flap over.

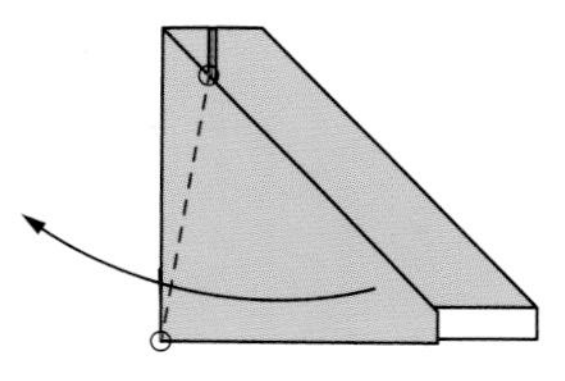

23 Valley fold the flap back over.

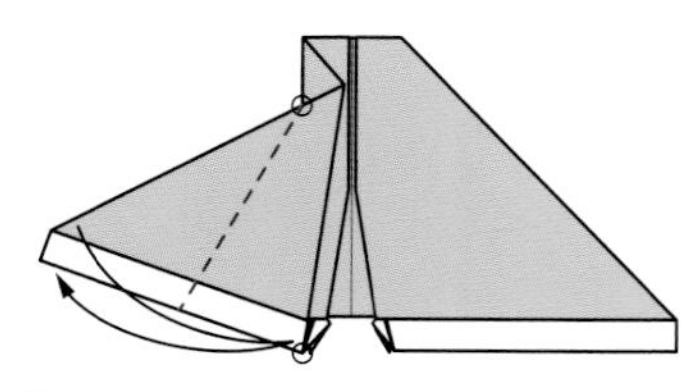

24 Fold and unfold as indicated.

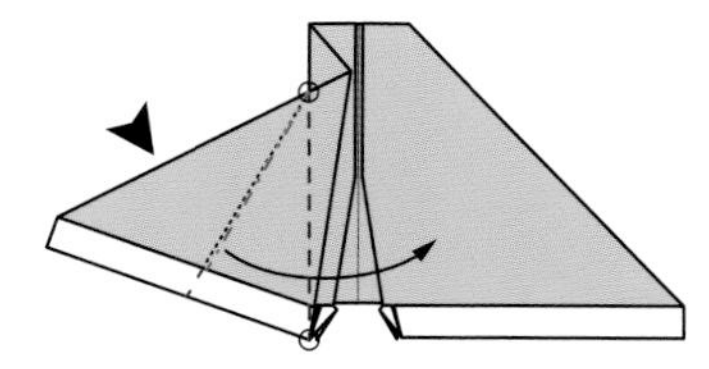

25 Squash fold on the existing crease. One new crease will form.

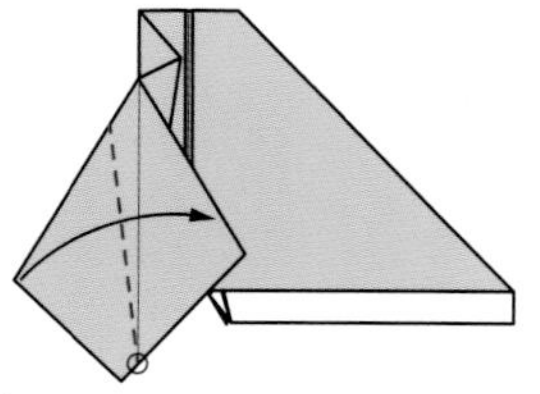

26 Valley fold as shown.

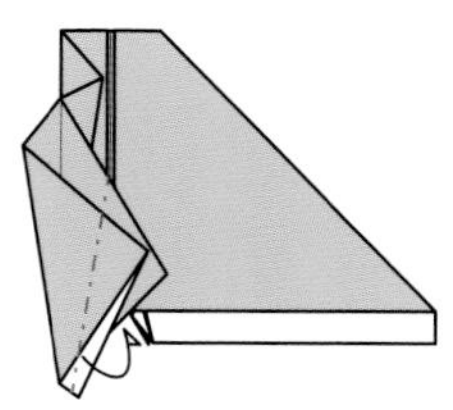

27 Mountain fold along the edge formed in step 21.

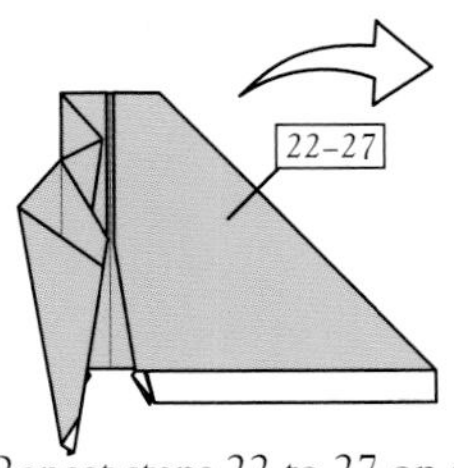

28 Repeat steps 22 to 27 on the other side.

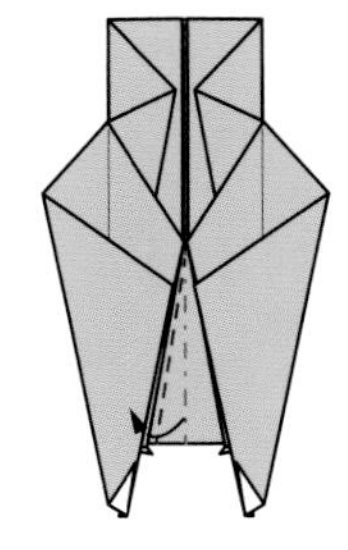

29 Pleat as indicated, making a three-dimensional convex shape on the back.

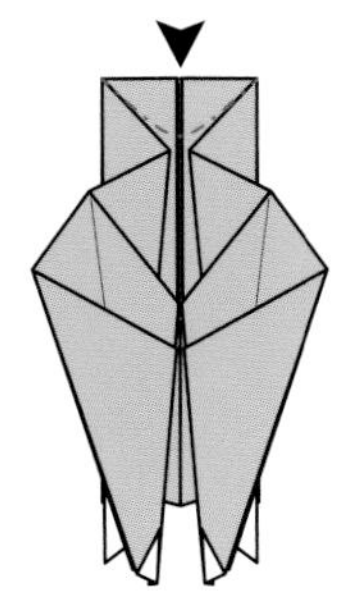

30 Round the head by pressing down as shown. Round the wings and body.

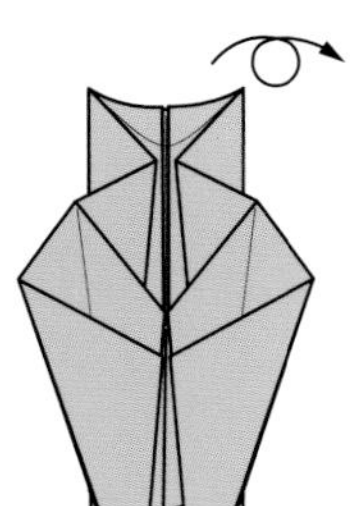

31 Turn over.

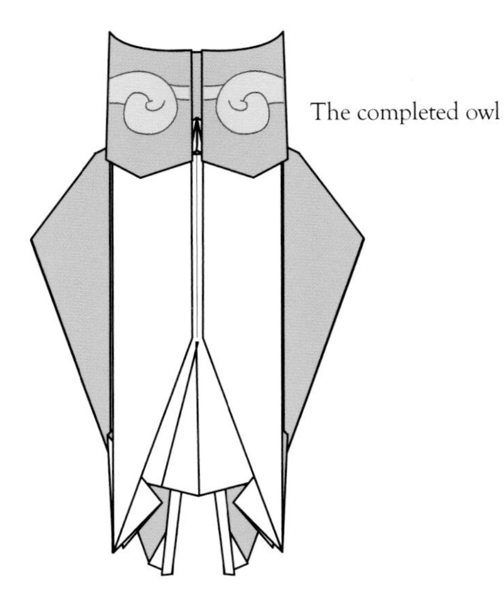

The completed owl

HORSE

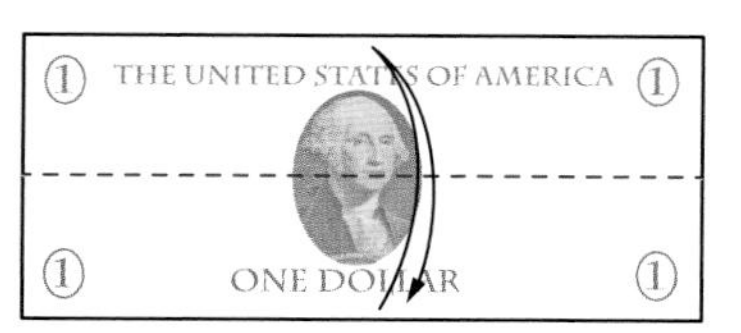

1 With the white (face) side up, valley fold the paper in half. Unfold.

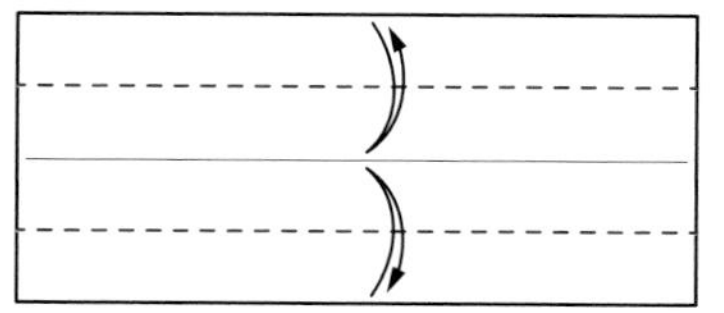

2 Fold in quarters. Unfold.

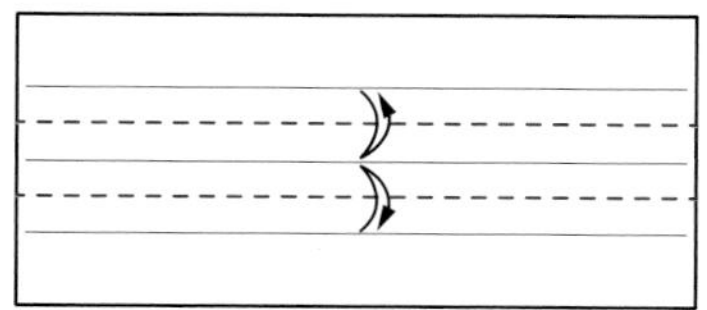

3 Fold between the crease lines. Unfold.

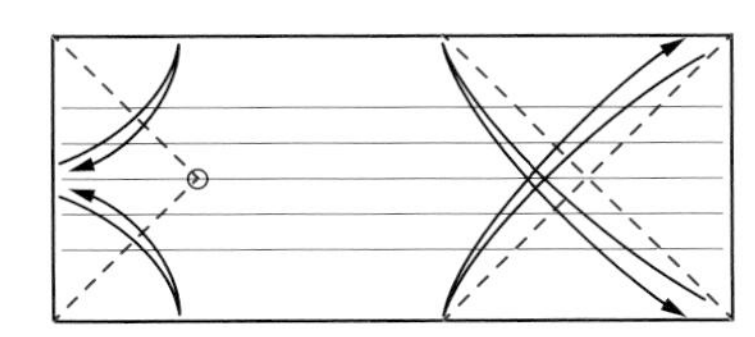

4 Fold the diagonals as indicated. Unfold.

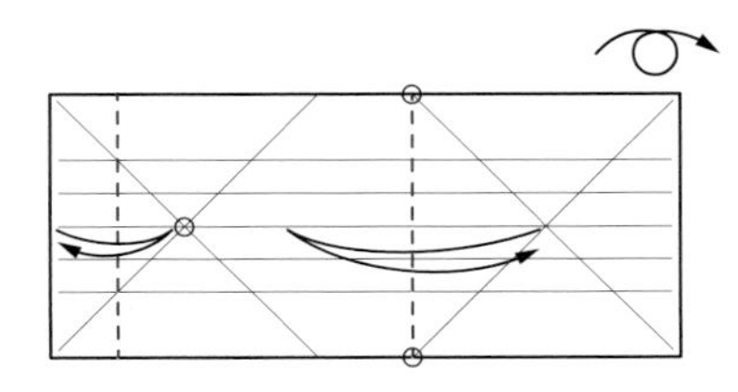

5 Fold the vertical creases as indicated. Unfold. Turn over.

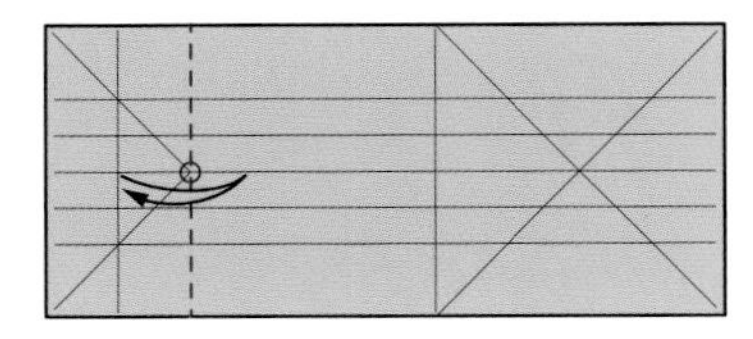

6 Fold vertically through the intersection of the creases. Unfold.

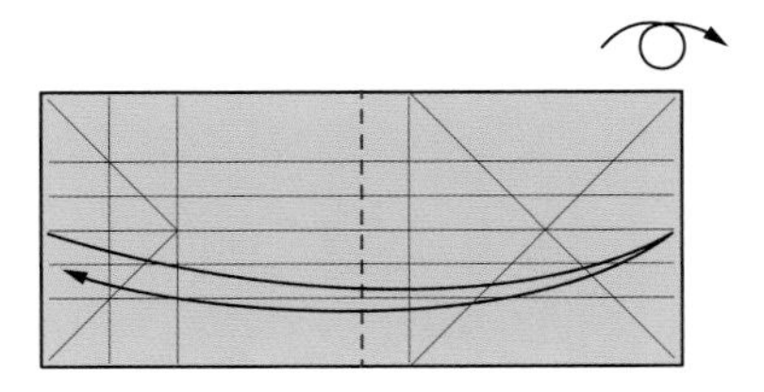

7 Fold in half. Unfold. Turn over.

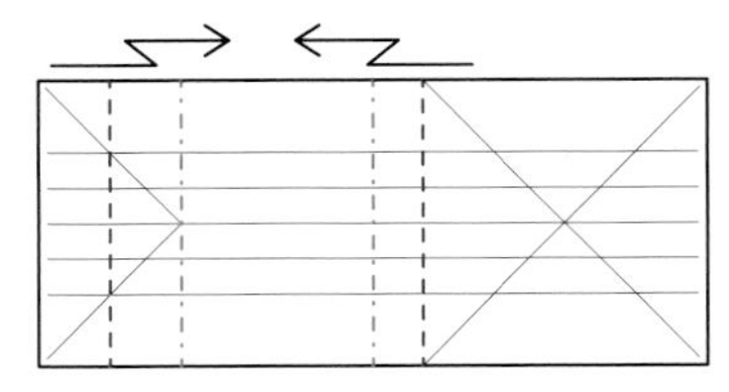

8 Pleat fold on existing creases.

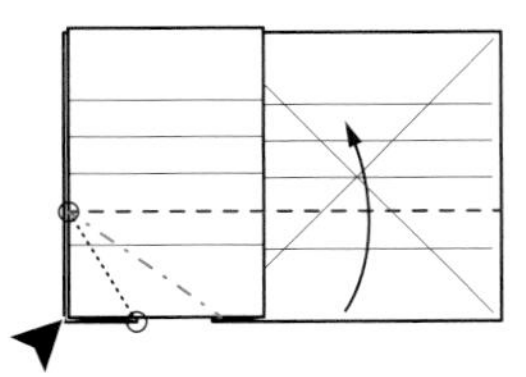

9 Squash the corner and swivel fold as shown.

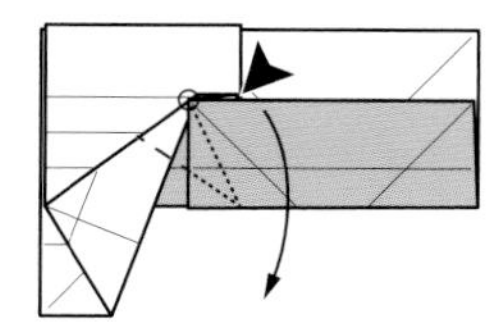

10 Squash and swivel fold.

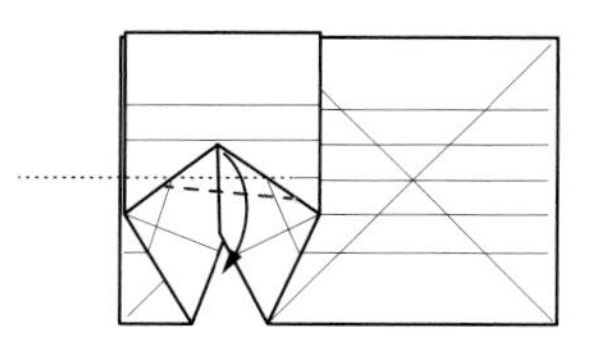

11 Fold the corner as indicated. Note that it is slanted and just below the center crease.

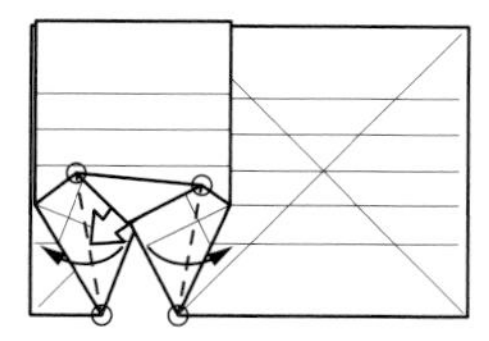

12 Pull out the trapped paper from inside and valley fold from corner to corner as shown.

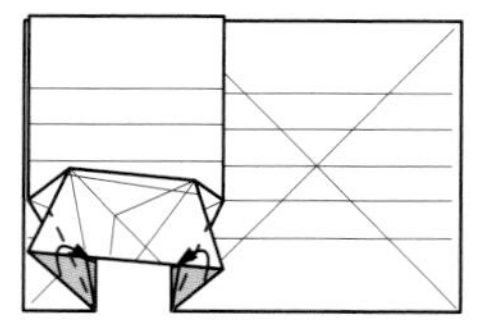

13 Fold the angle bisectors shown, matching raw edge to raw edge.

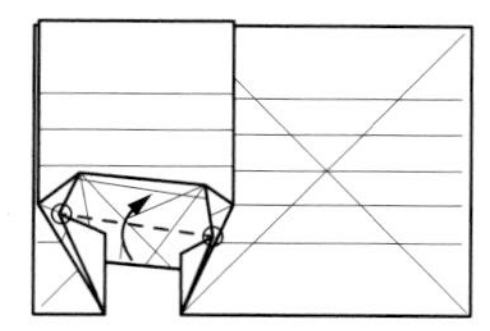

14 Fold corner to corner, pulling out the paper trapped inside.

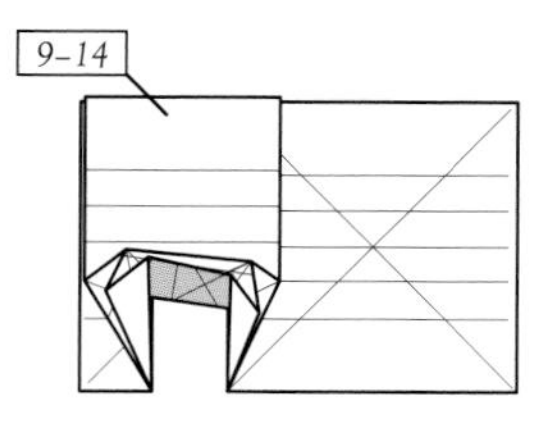

15 Repeat steps 9 to 14 on the other side.

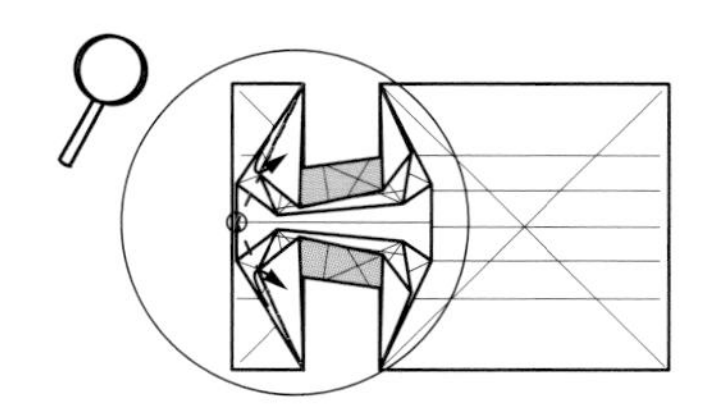

16 Valley fold the corners indicated. Detailed views are next.

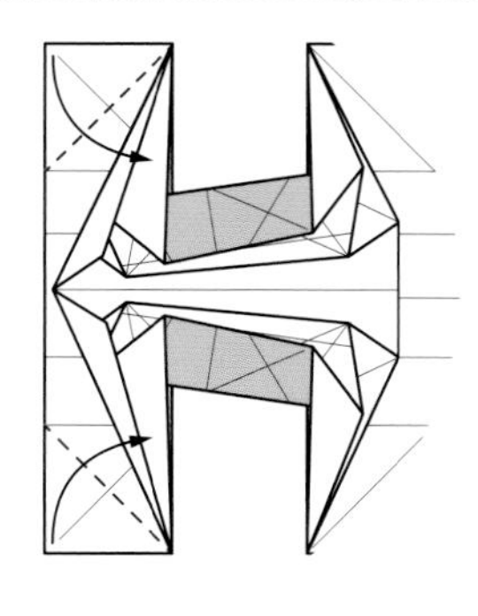

17 Valley fold as indicated.

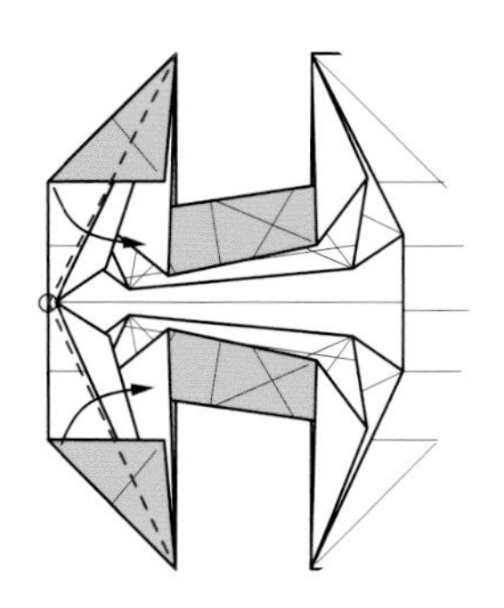

18 Valley fold as indicated.

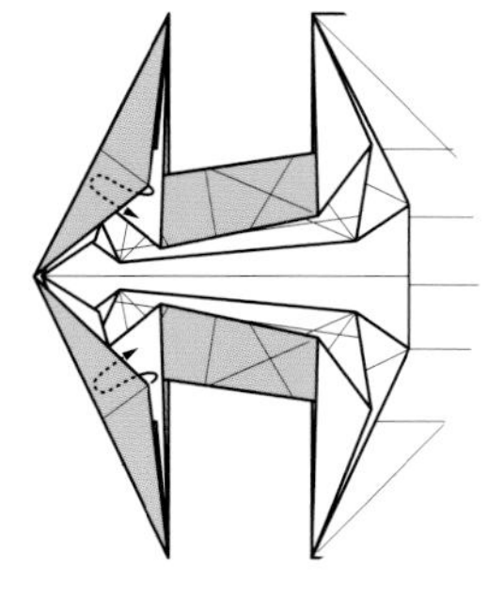

19 Tuck the triangular flaps inside.

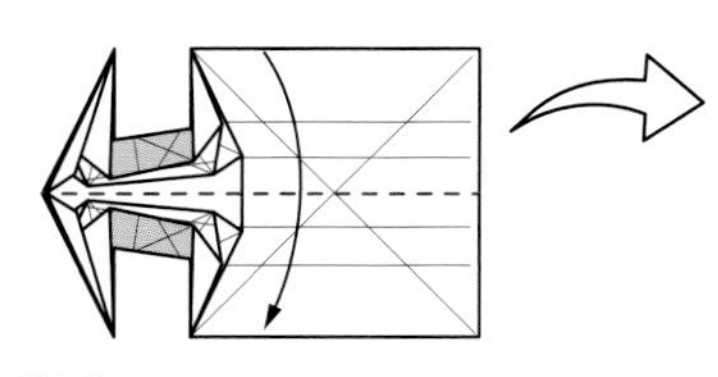

20 Fold the entire model in half.

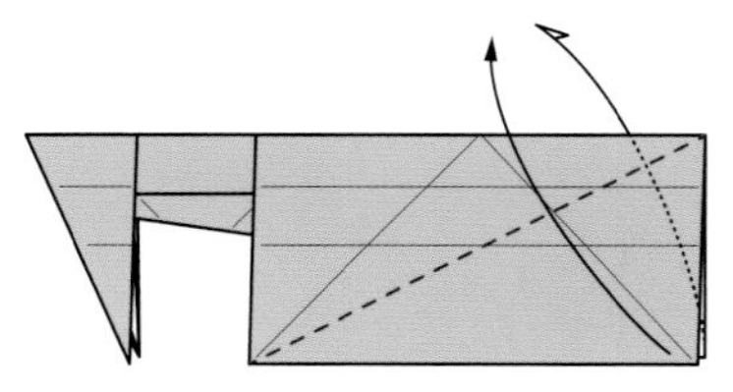

21 Fold corner to corner on both the front and back flaps.

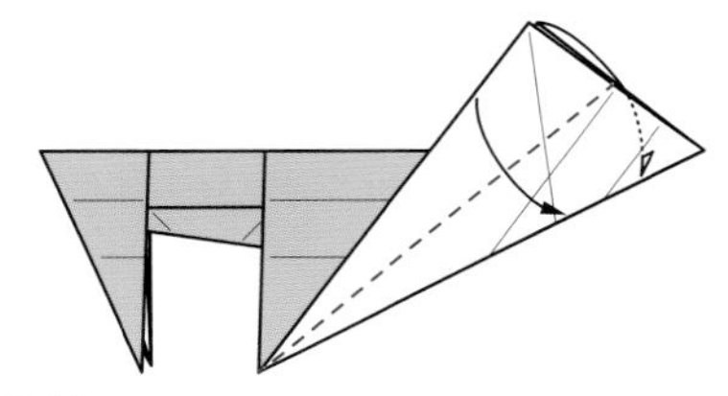

22 Fold an angle bisector, edge to edge, on the front and back flaps.

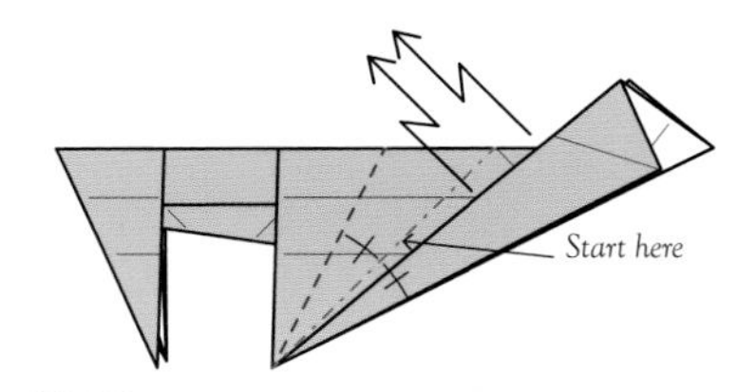

23 Crimp fold: Start with the existing mountain crease and then create the valley crease along the edge. See next step for the result.

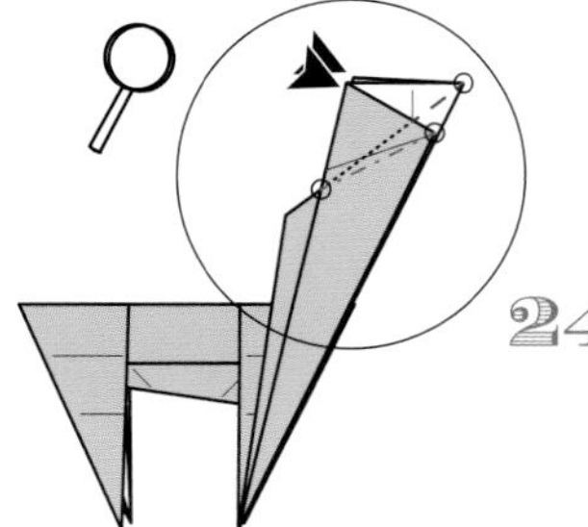

24 Reverse fold as indicated on the front and back corners.

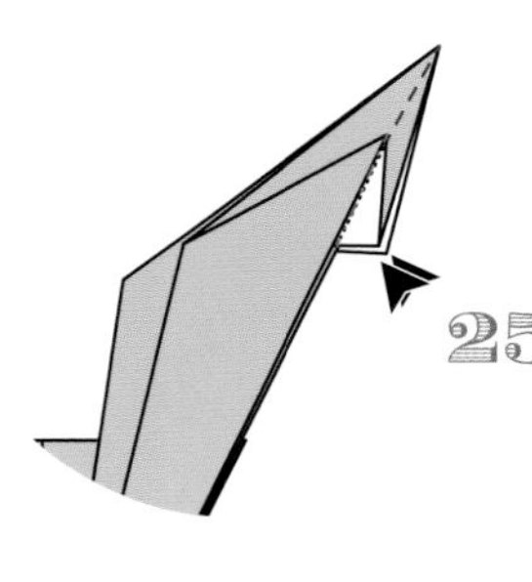

25 Reverse fold as indicated on the front and back corners.

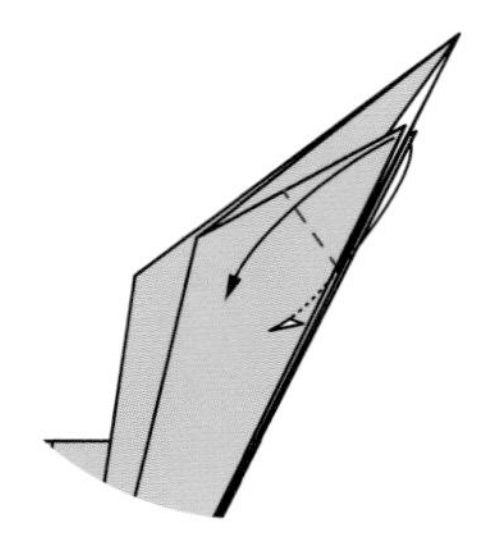

26 Fold the flaps down on the front and back as far as they can go.

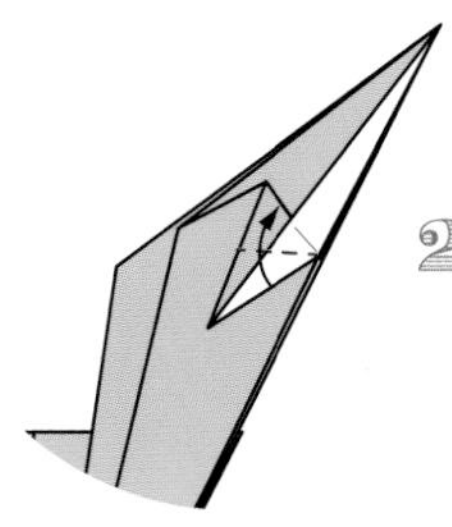

27 Valley fold the angle bisector. Repeat on the back.

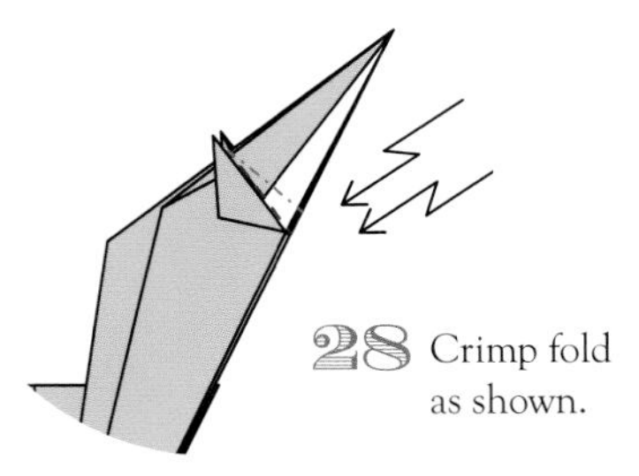

28 Crimp fold as shown.

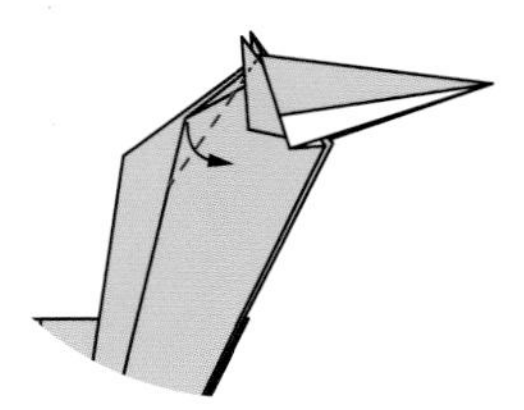

29 Valley fold as shown. Repeat on the back layer.

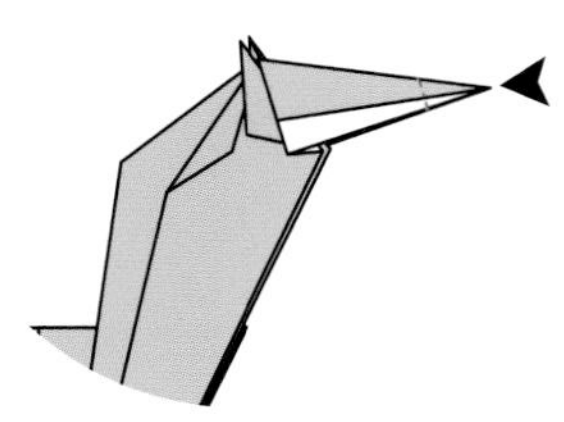

30 Open sink the nose tip.

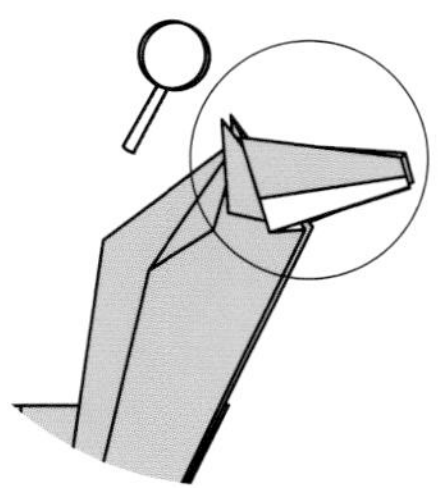

31 Detailed view of the head is next.

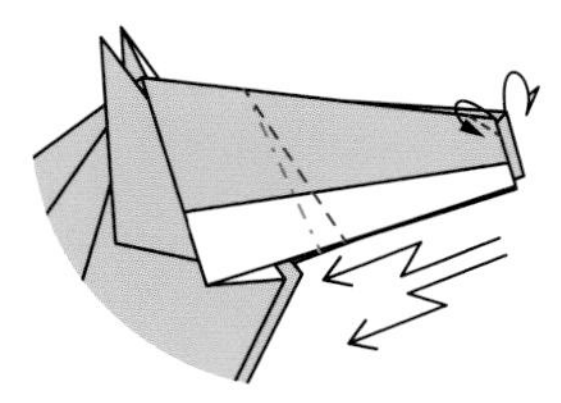

32 Valley fold to define the nostrils, then crimp to define the face.

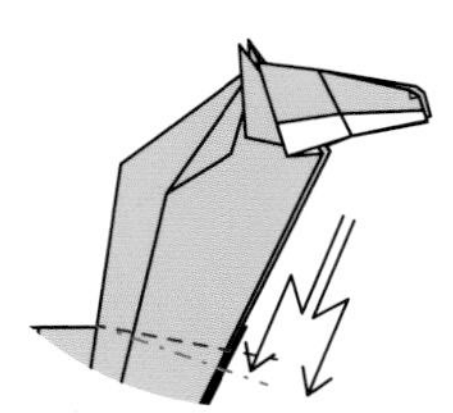

33 Crimp at the base of the neck as shown.

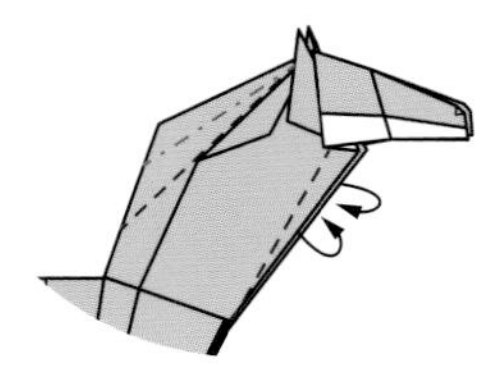

34 Narrow the neck by folding the edges inside, then crease as shown to form the mane.

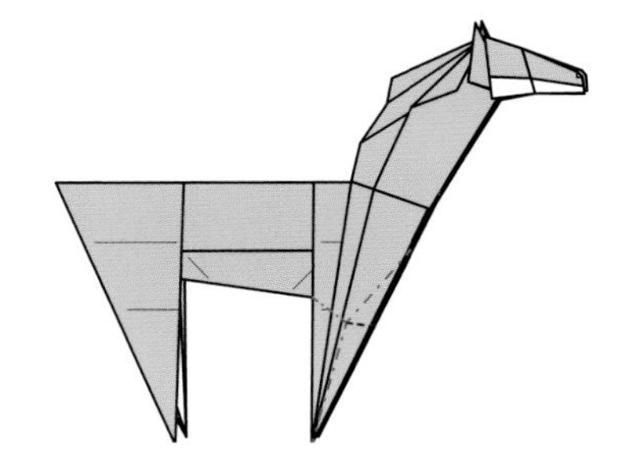

35 Rabbit-ear to narrow and shape both forelegs.

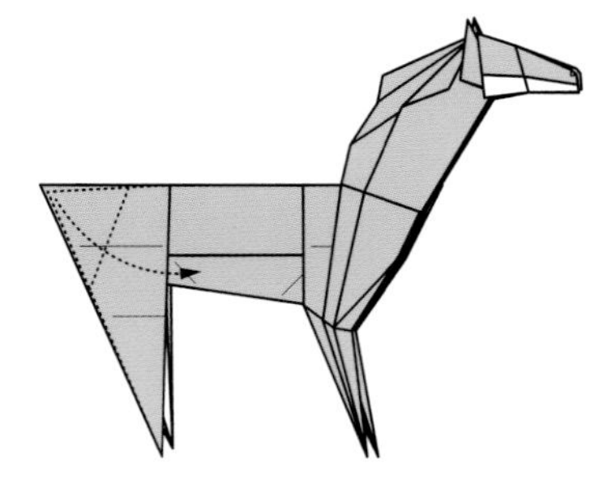

36 Reverse fold the inner corner (created in step 16) as indicated.

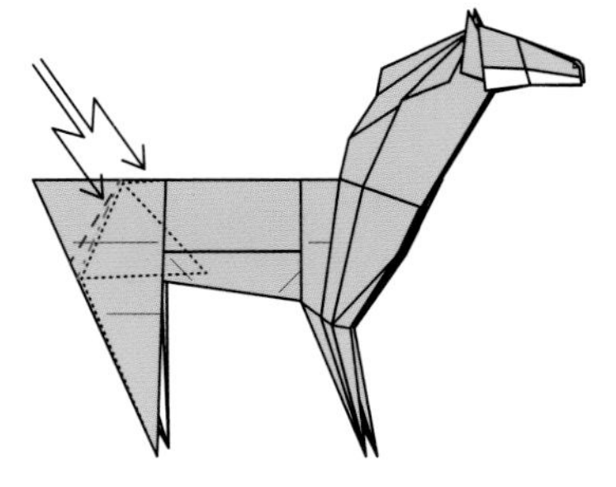

37 Crimp to define the tail.

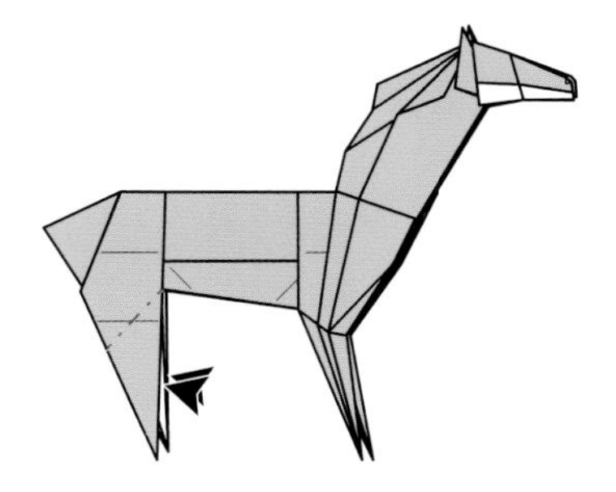

38 Reverse fold the hind legs.

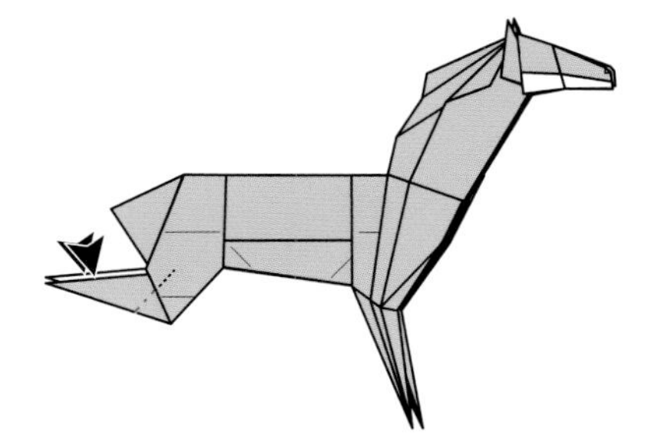

39 Reverse fold the legs.

40 Pleat the tail as shown.

The completed horse

GUITAR

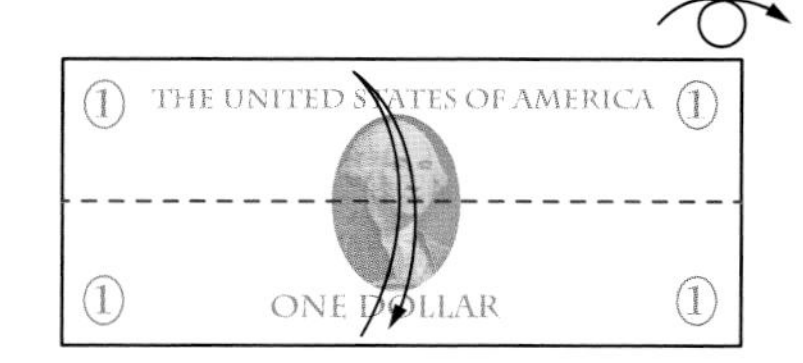

1 With the white (face) side up, fold in half horizontally. Unfold. Turn over.

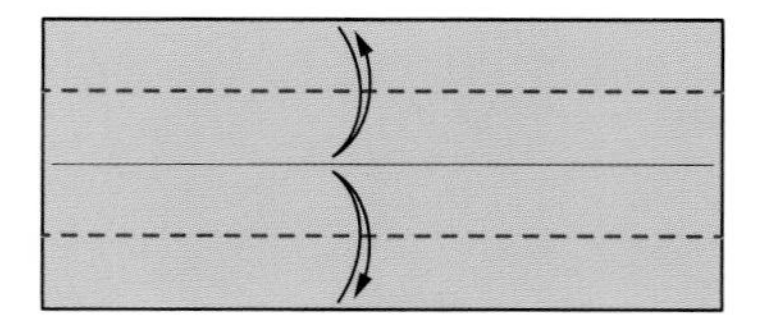

2 Fold in quarters. Unfold.

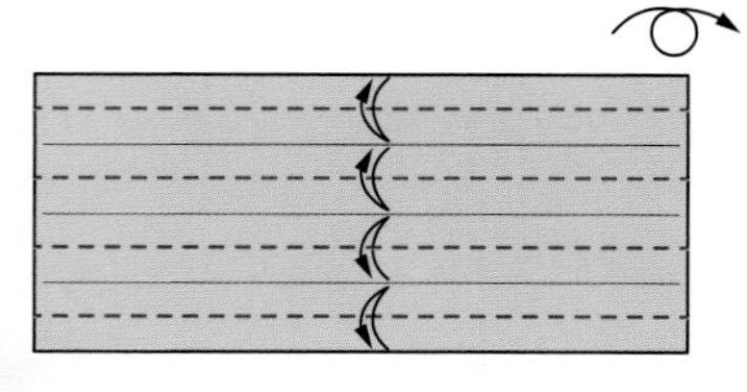

3 Fold in eighths. Unfold. Turn over.

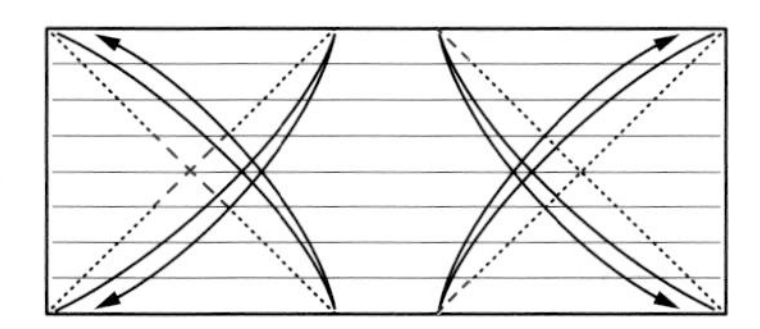

4 Fold the diagonals shown, creasing only where indicated.

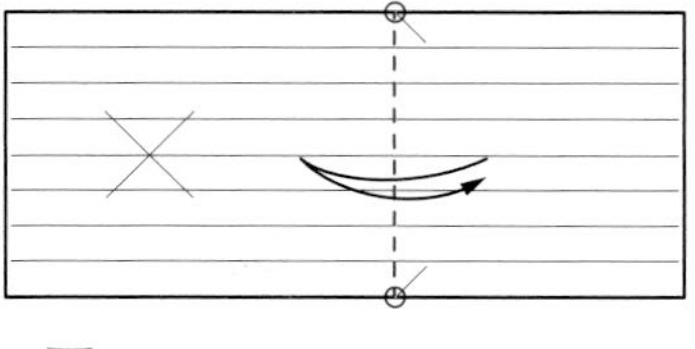

5 Crease vertically between the reference points.

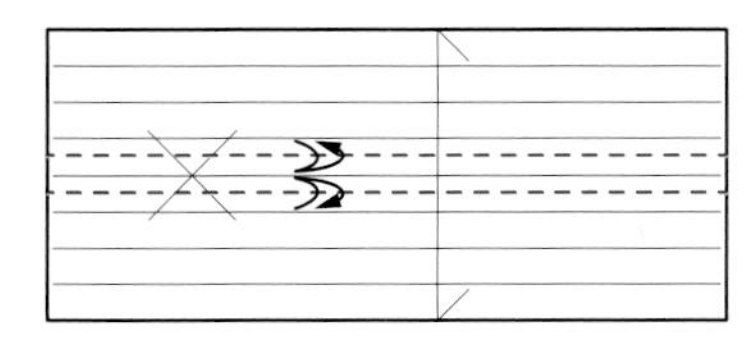

6 Crease between the creases.

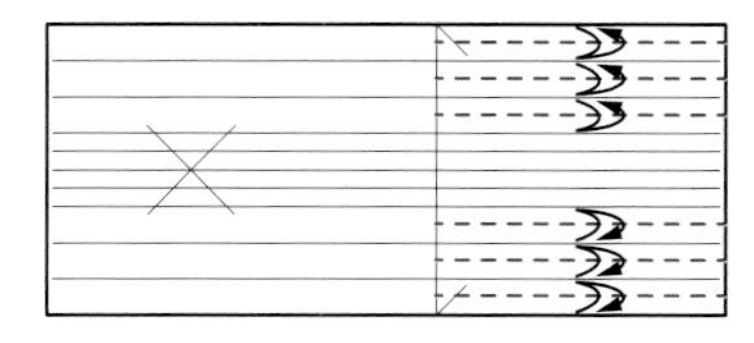

7 Crease between the creases.

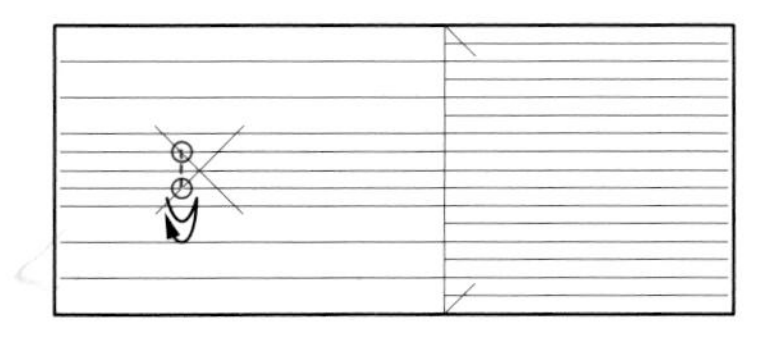

8 Crease vertically between the reference points.

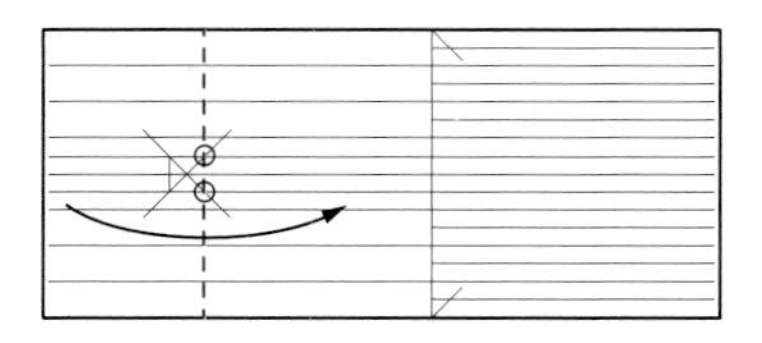

9 Valley fold vertically through the references points indicated. Turn over from top to bottom.

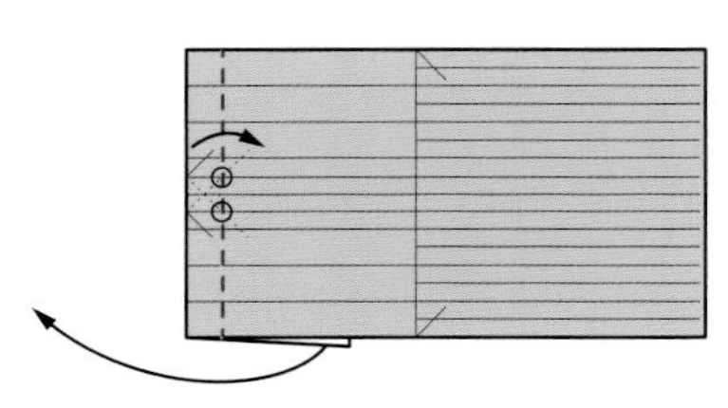

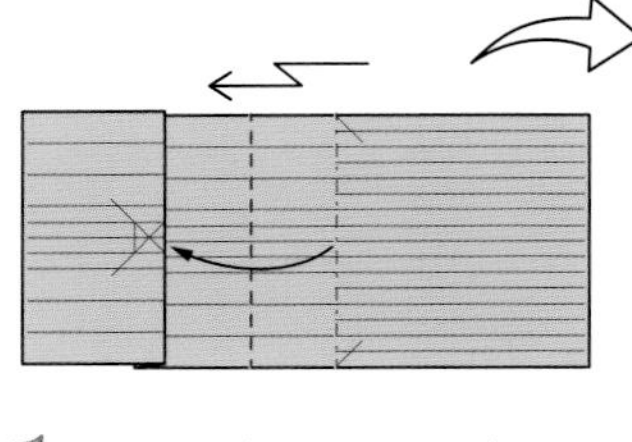

10 Valley fold using the short crease on the bottom layer (made in step 8) as a reference; let the flap flip out, creating a pleat.

11 Pleat fold as shown. The next steps will involve a sequence of swivels to narrow the neck.

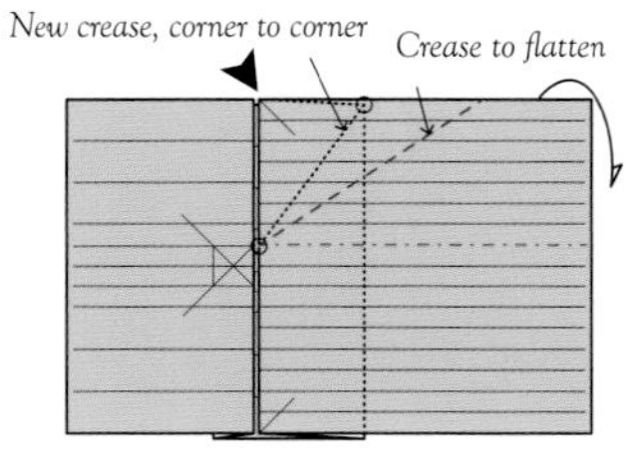

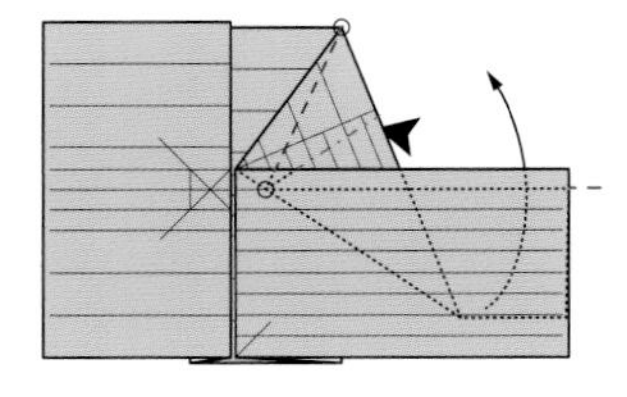

12 Mountain fold the flap behind on the existing horizontal crease. Make new creases as indicated to make it flat.

13 Valley fold the flap up on the existing horizontal crease. Make new creases as indicated to make it flat.

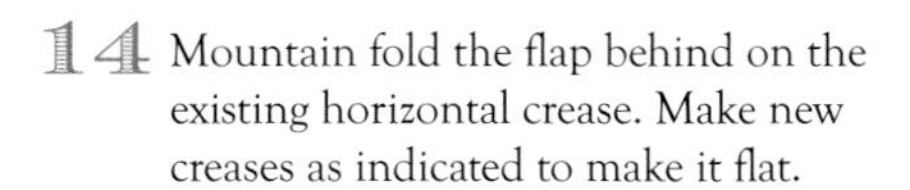

14 Mountain fold the flap behind on the existing horizontal crease. Make new creases as indicated to make it flat.

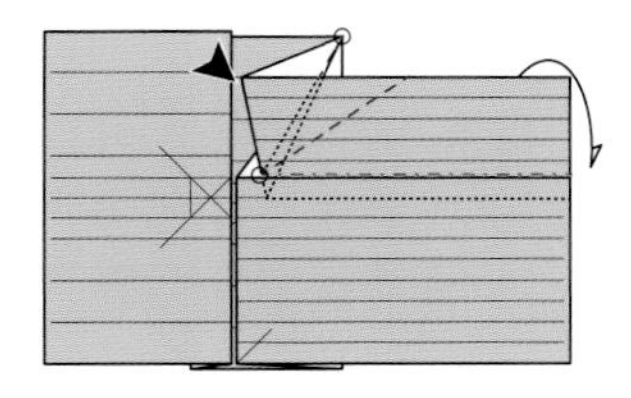

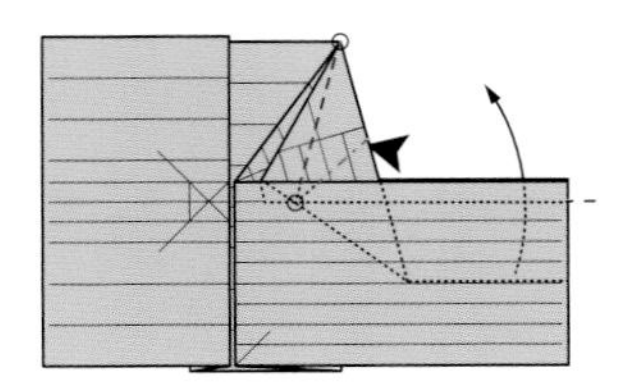

15 Valley fold the flap up on the existing horizontal crease. Make new creases as indicated to make it flat.

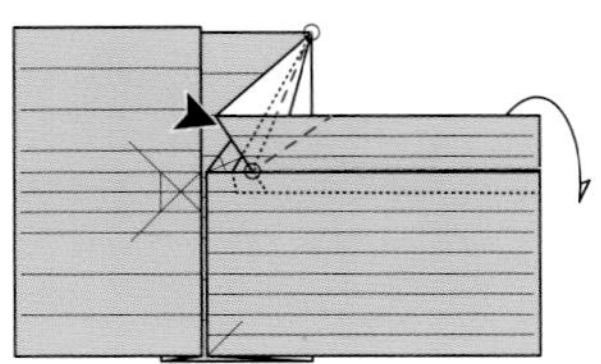

16 Mountain fold the flap behind on the existing horizontal crease. Make new creases as indicated to make it flat.

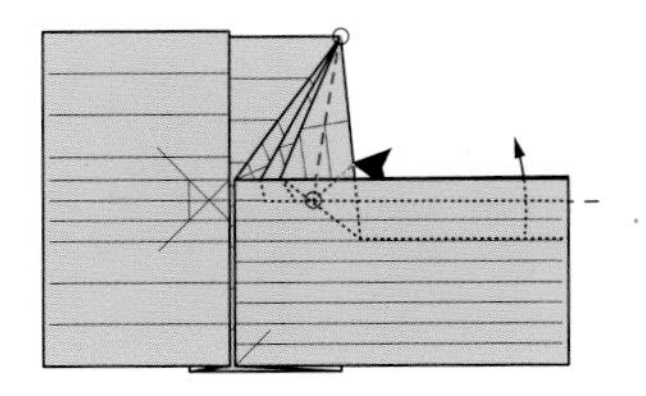

17 Valley fold the flap up on the existing horizontal crease. Make new creases as indicated to make it flat.

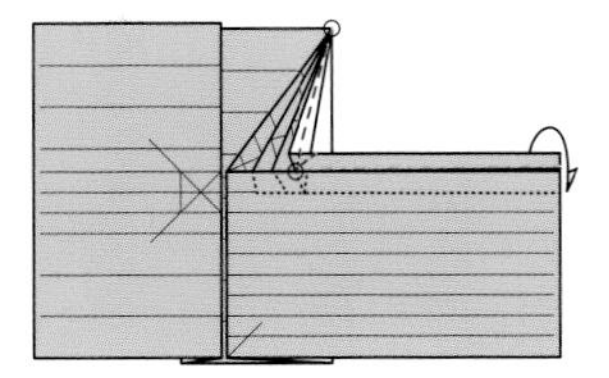

18 Mountain fold the flap behind on the existing horizontal crease. Make new creases as indicated to make it flat.

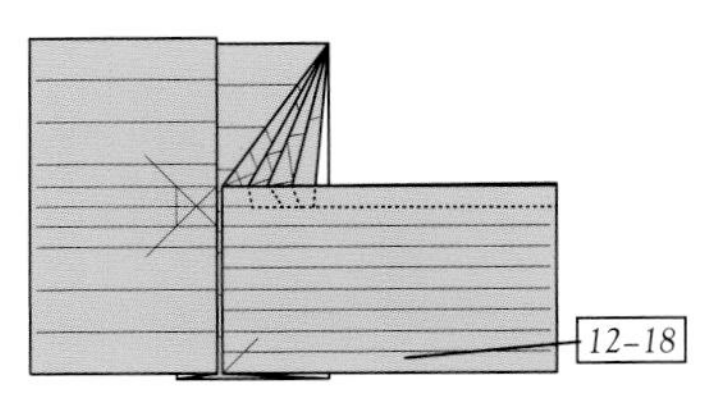

19 Repeat steps 12 to 18 on the other side.

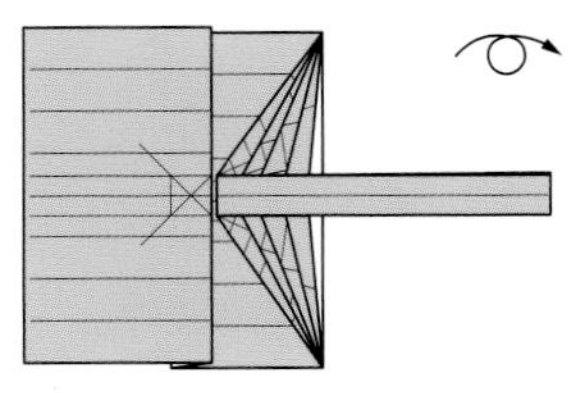

20 Turn over.

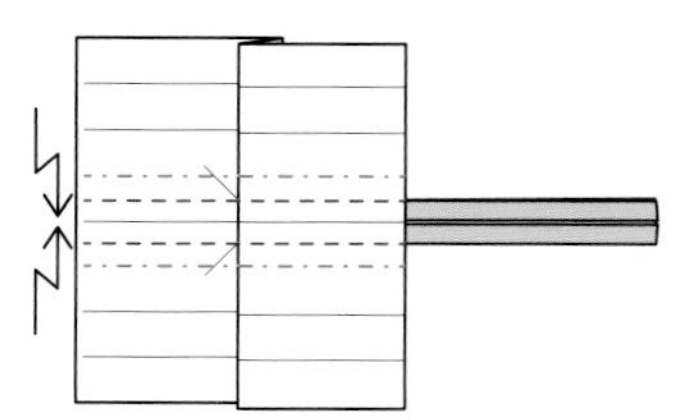

21 Pleat fold as shown.

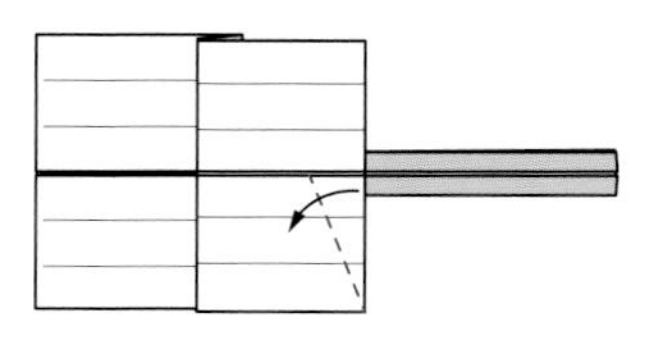

22 Shape the guitar body with swivels: Start with a valley fold. The model will not lie flat. See next step.

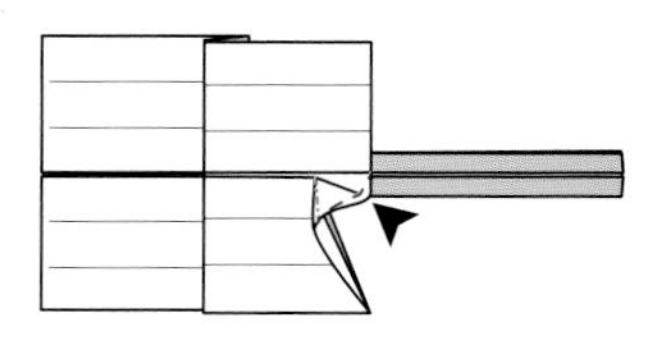

23 Swivel and squash, making it flat.

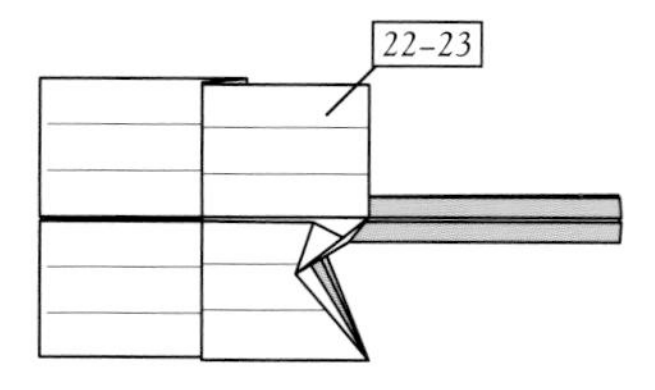

24 Repeat steps 22 to 23 on the other side.

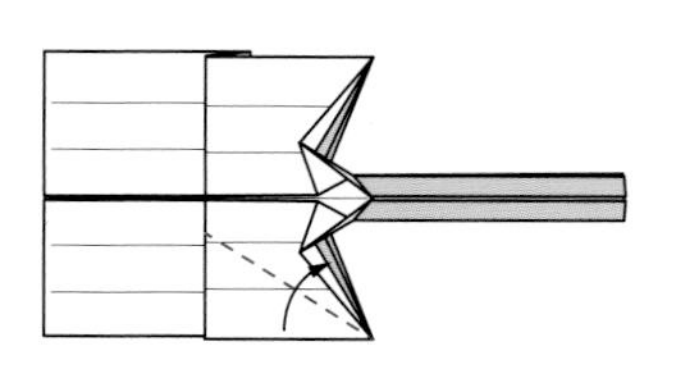

25 Continue shaping with swivels: Start with a valley fold. The model will not lie flat.

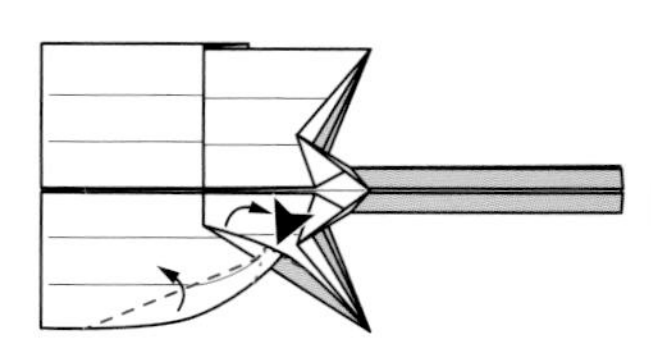

26 Swivel and squash, making it flat.

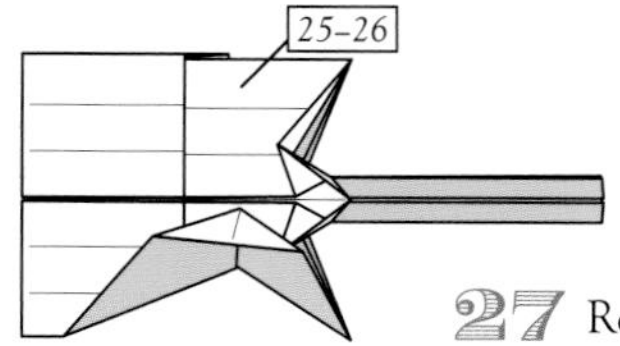

27 Repeat steps 25 and 26 on the other side.

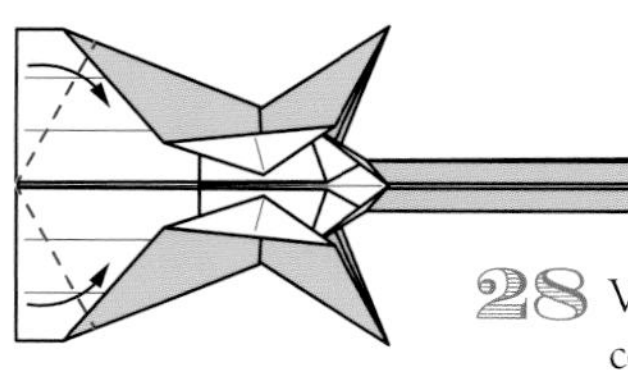

28 Valley fold the corners to the creases indicated.

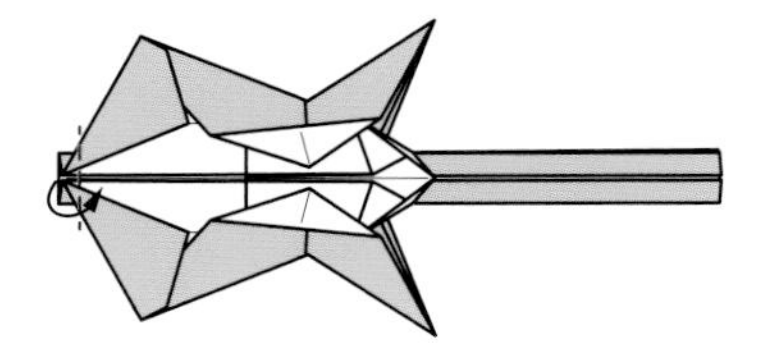

29 Valley fold the extra paper over.

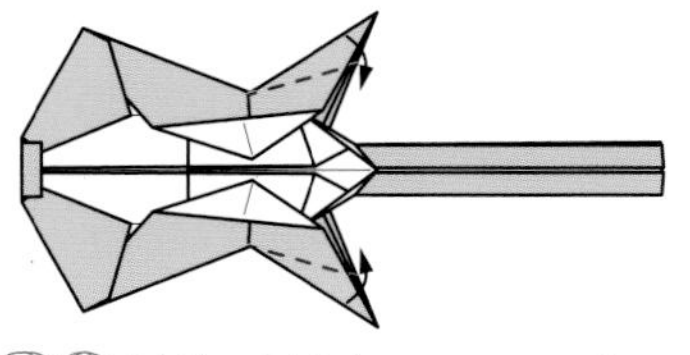

30 Valley fold the points as shown.

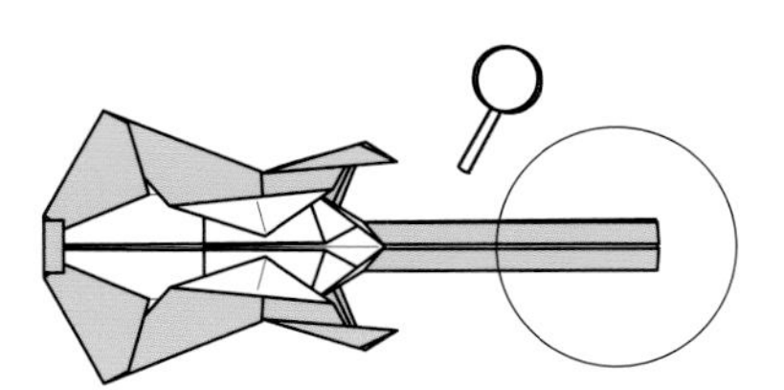

31 Details of the head and pegs are next.

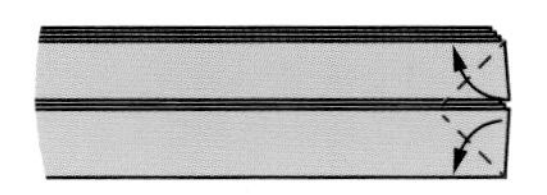

32 Valley fold the top layer as shown.

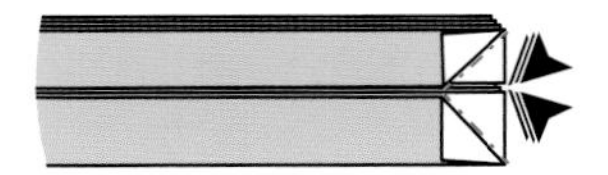

33 Reverse fold the three corners on the top and the three corners on the bottom.

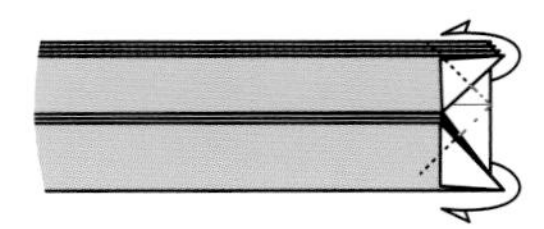

34 Mountain fold the last layer, creating a corner.

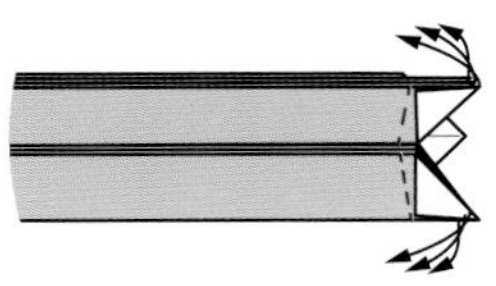

35 Valley fold the corners as indicated, spreading them apart evenly. See next step for expected result.

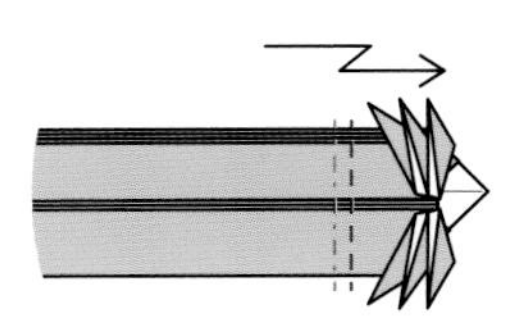

36 Pleat through all layers.

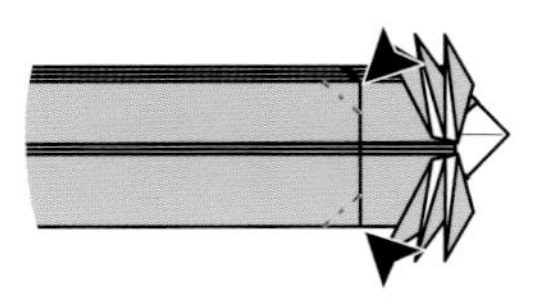

37 Push the corners in.

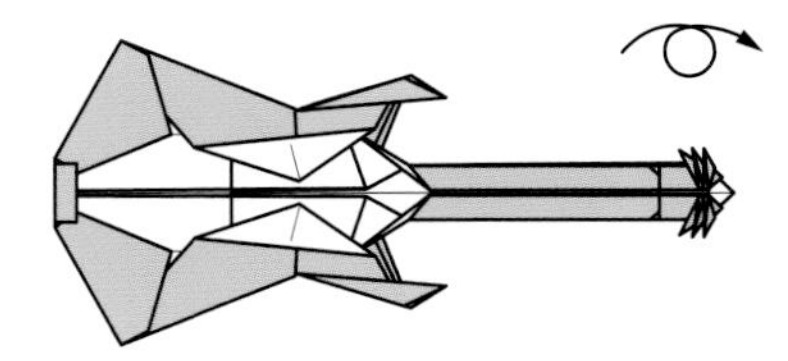

38 Turn the model over.

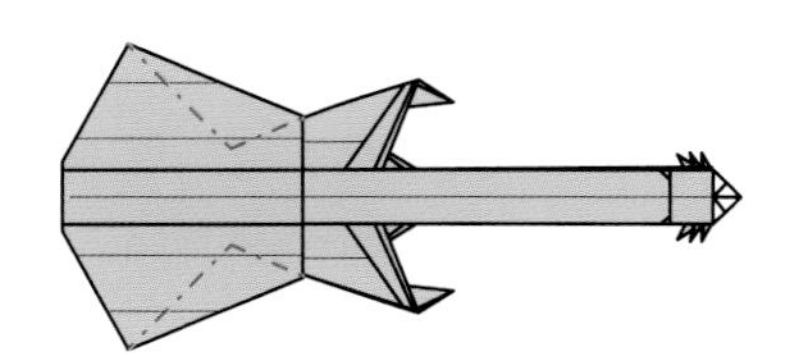

39 Mountain crease as shown for the final shaping.

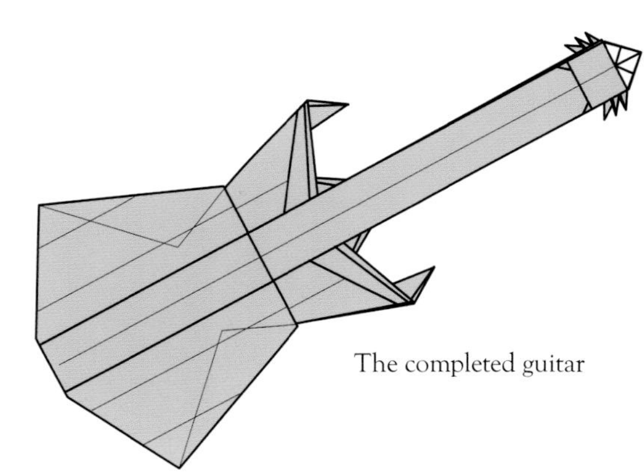

The completed guitar

ROOSTER

1 With the green (back) side up, fold the bill in half horizontally and vertically. Unfold after each fold. Turn over.

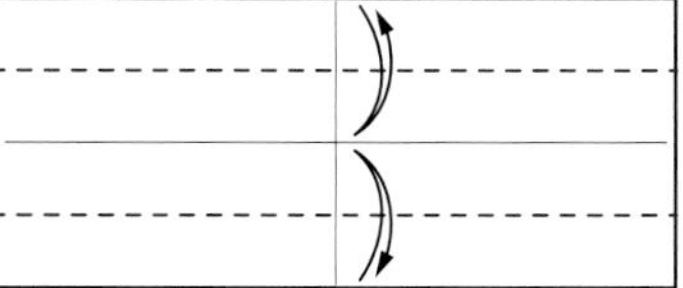

2 Valley fold horizontally in quarters. Unfold.

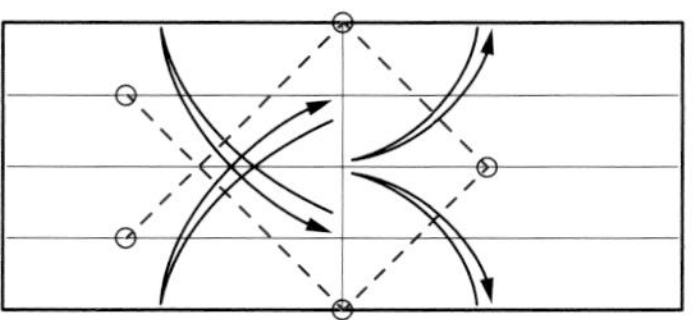

3 Valley fold the diagonals indicated. Unfold.

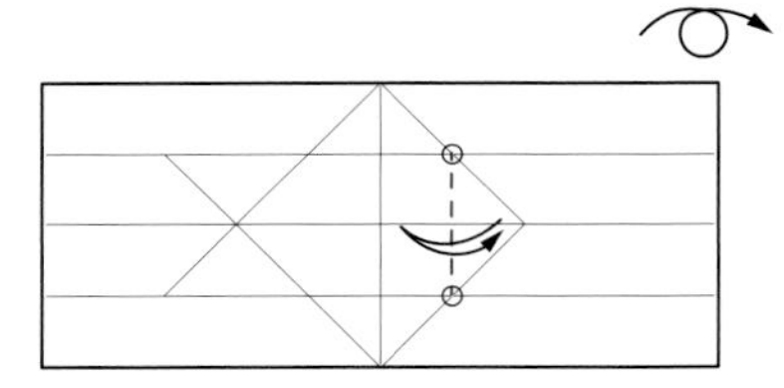

4 Fold between the reference points indicated. Unfold. Turn over.

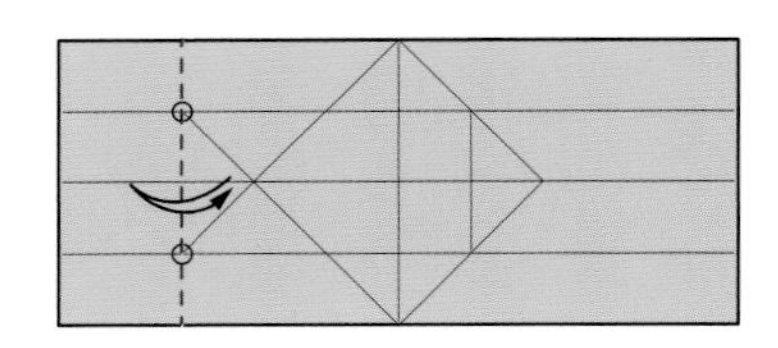

5 Fold through the reference points indicated and unfold.

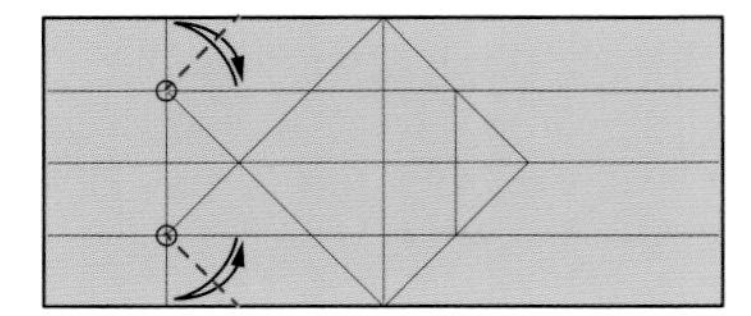

6 Fold the edges to the creases shown, creasing diagonals. Unfold.

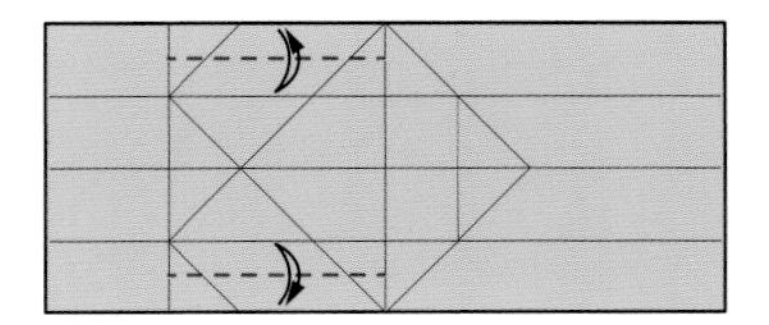

7 Fold the edges to the creases shown. Unfold.

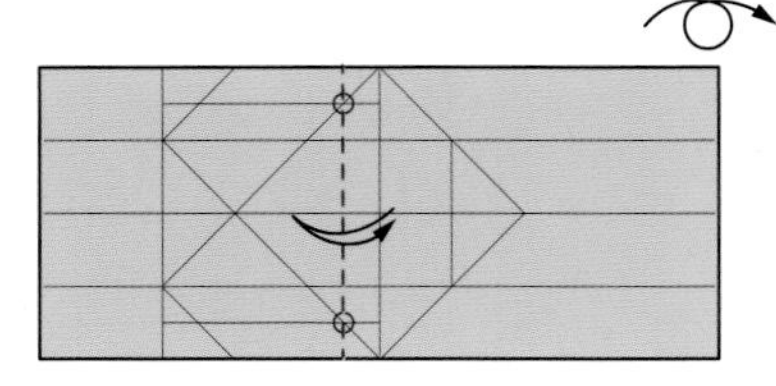

8 Fold through the reference points indicated. Unfold. Turn over.

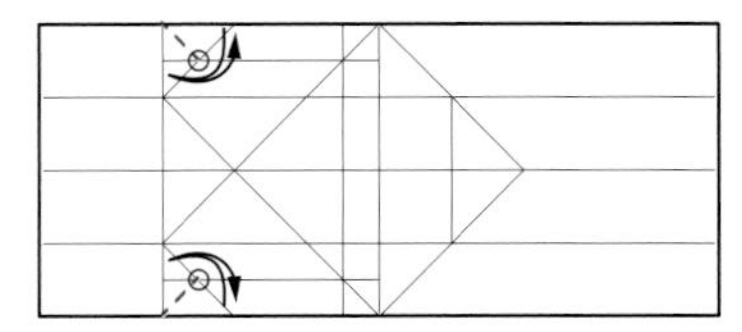

9 Fold the edges to the creases indicated, creasing diagonals. Unfold.

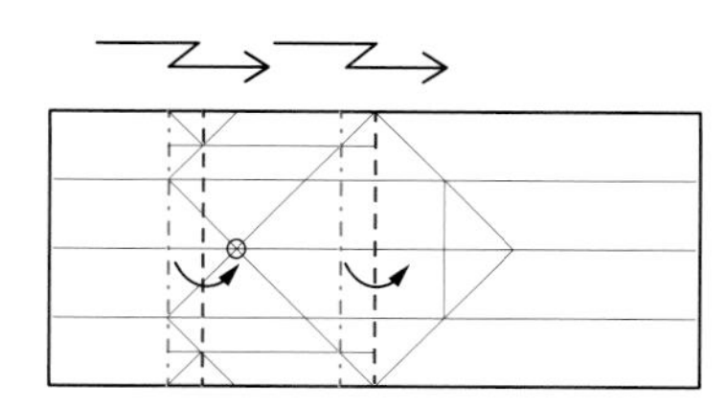

10 Pleat as indicated.

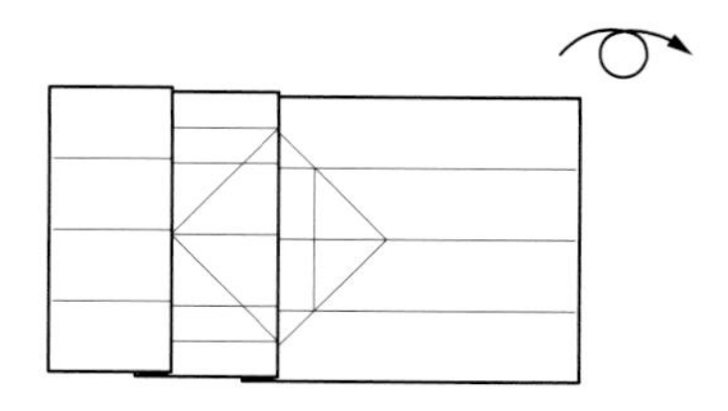

11 Turn over.

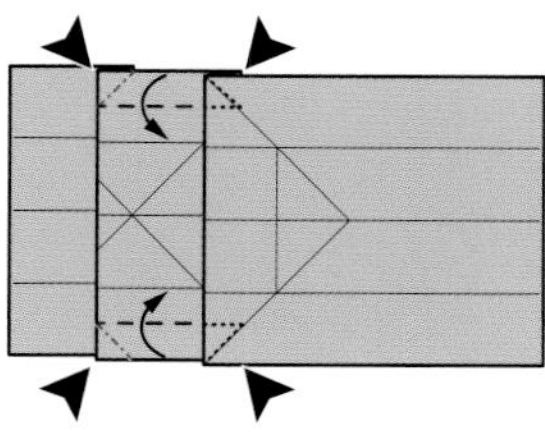

12 Fold the edges inward to the crease lines, squashing the corners.

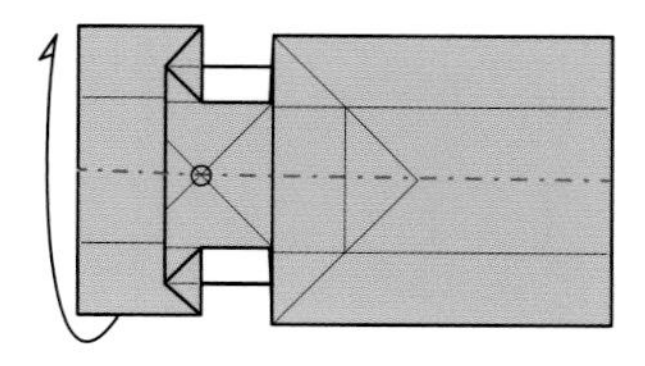

13 Mountain fold the model in half.

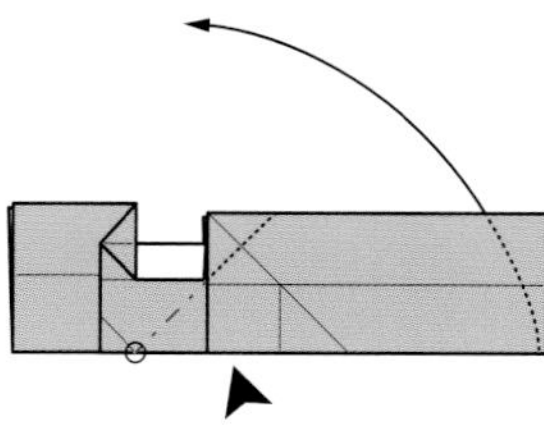

14 Reverse fold.

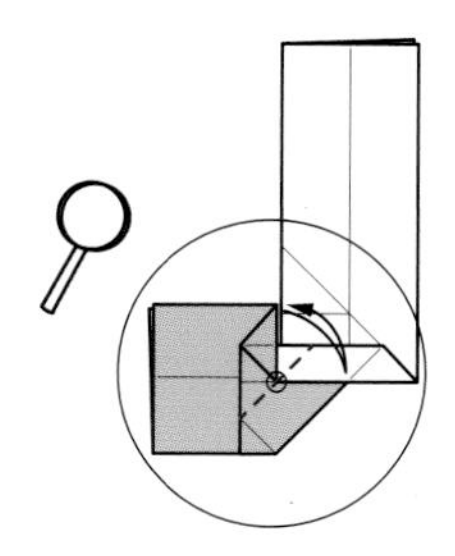

15 Fold the diagonal shown and unfold.

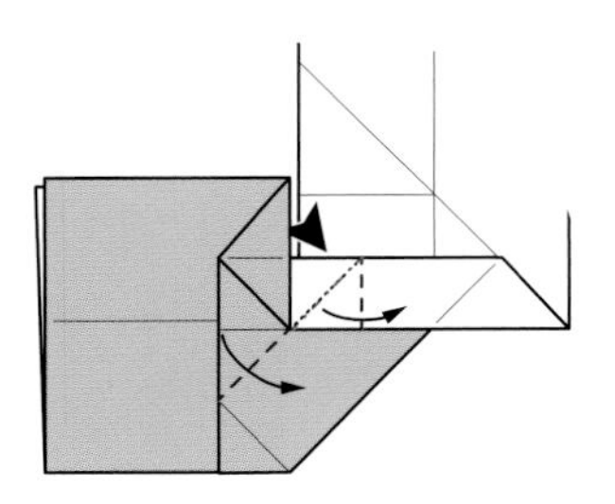

16 Squash using existing creases. The model will not lie flat. See next step for expected result.

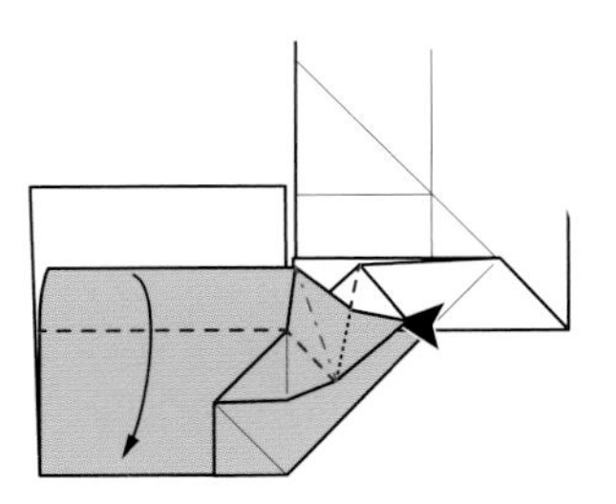

17 Continue the collapse as indicated. Fold the flap down and squash the paper to flatten.

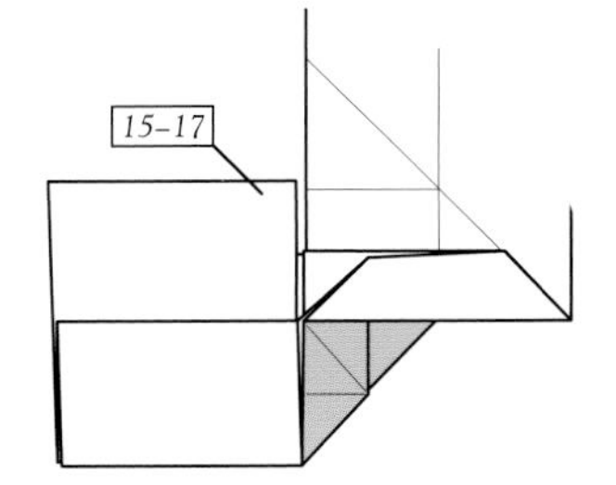

18 Repeat steps 15 to 17 on the other side.

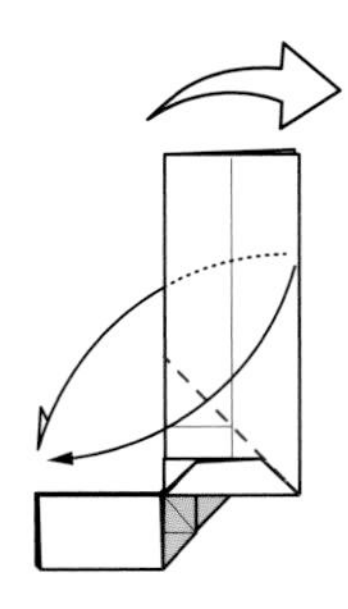

19 Outside reverse fold.

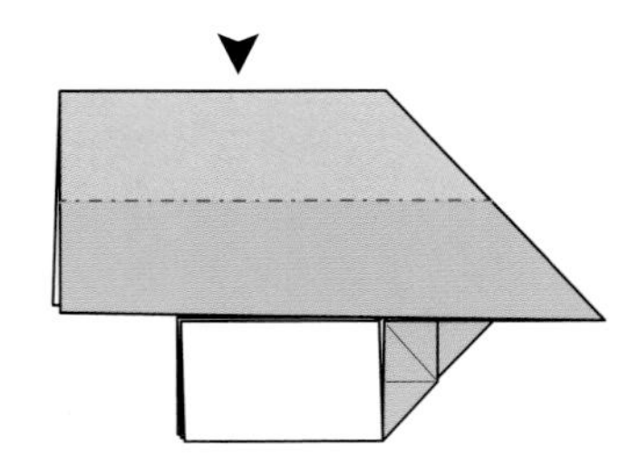

20 Open sink the area indicated.

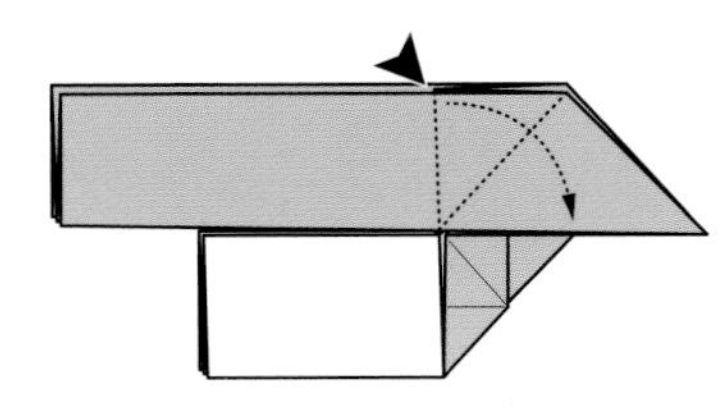

21 Reverse the corner hidden between the layers.

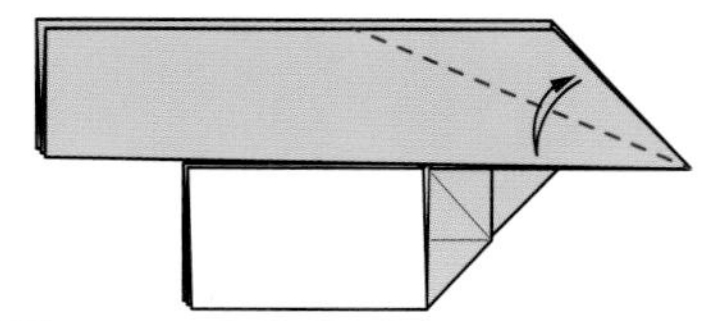

22 Fold the angle bisector, creasing well (the layers are thick here). Unfold.

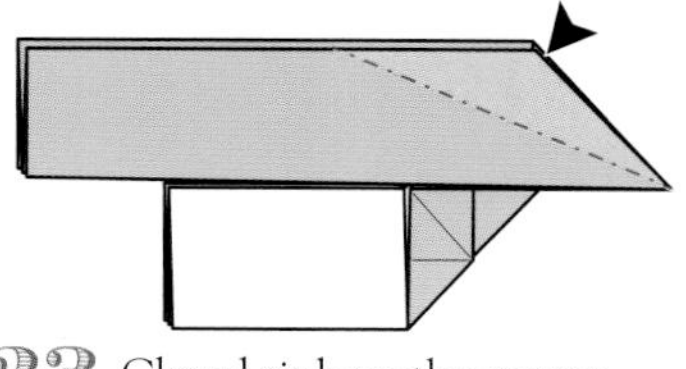

23 Closed sink on the creases formed in the previous step.

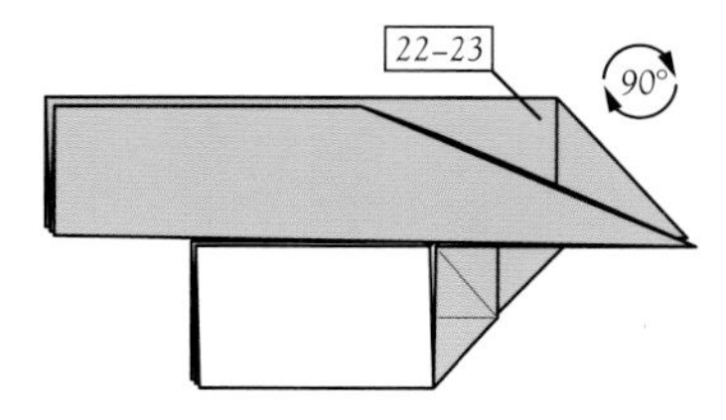

24 Repeat steps 22 to 23 on the other side. Rotate 90°.

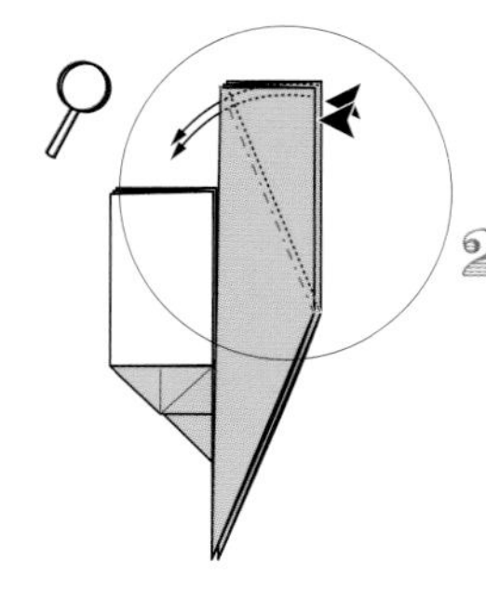

25 Reverse fold the two corners.

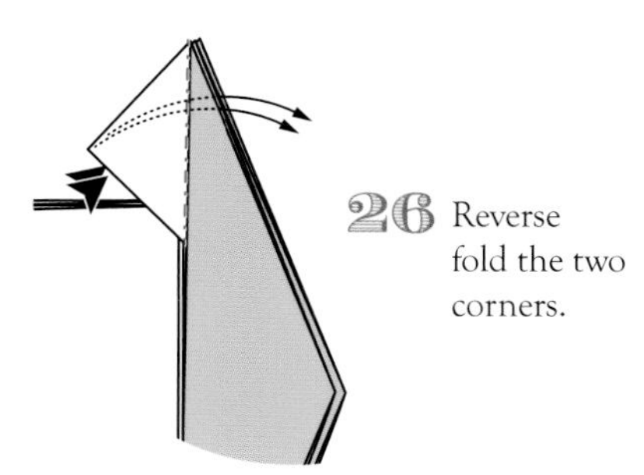

26 Reverse fold the two corners.

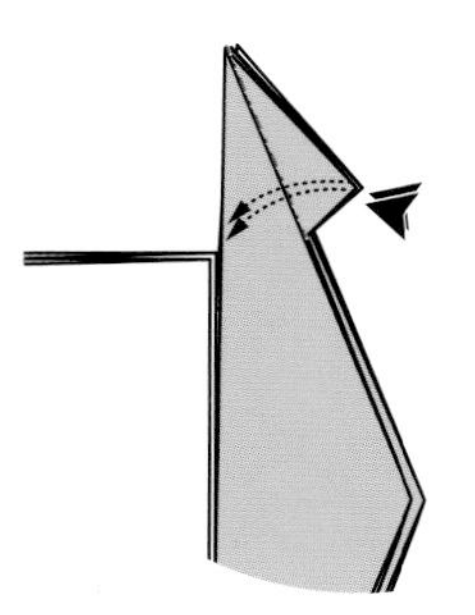

27 Reverse fold the two corners one last time.

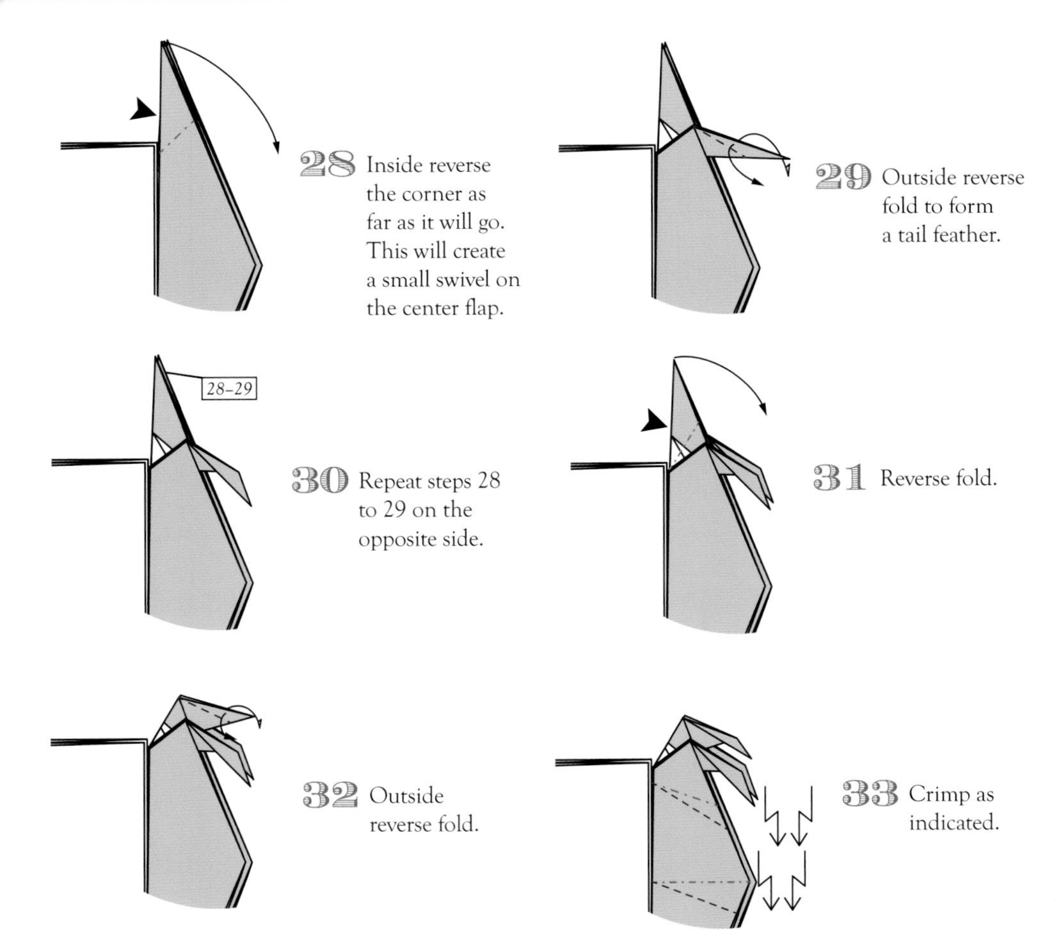

28 Inside reverse the corner as far as it will go. This will create a small swivel on the center flap.

29 Outside reverse fold to form a tail feather.

30 Repeat steps 28 to 29 on the opposite side.

31 Reverse fold.

32 Outside reverse fold.

33 Crimp as indicated.

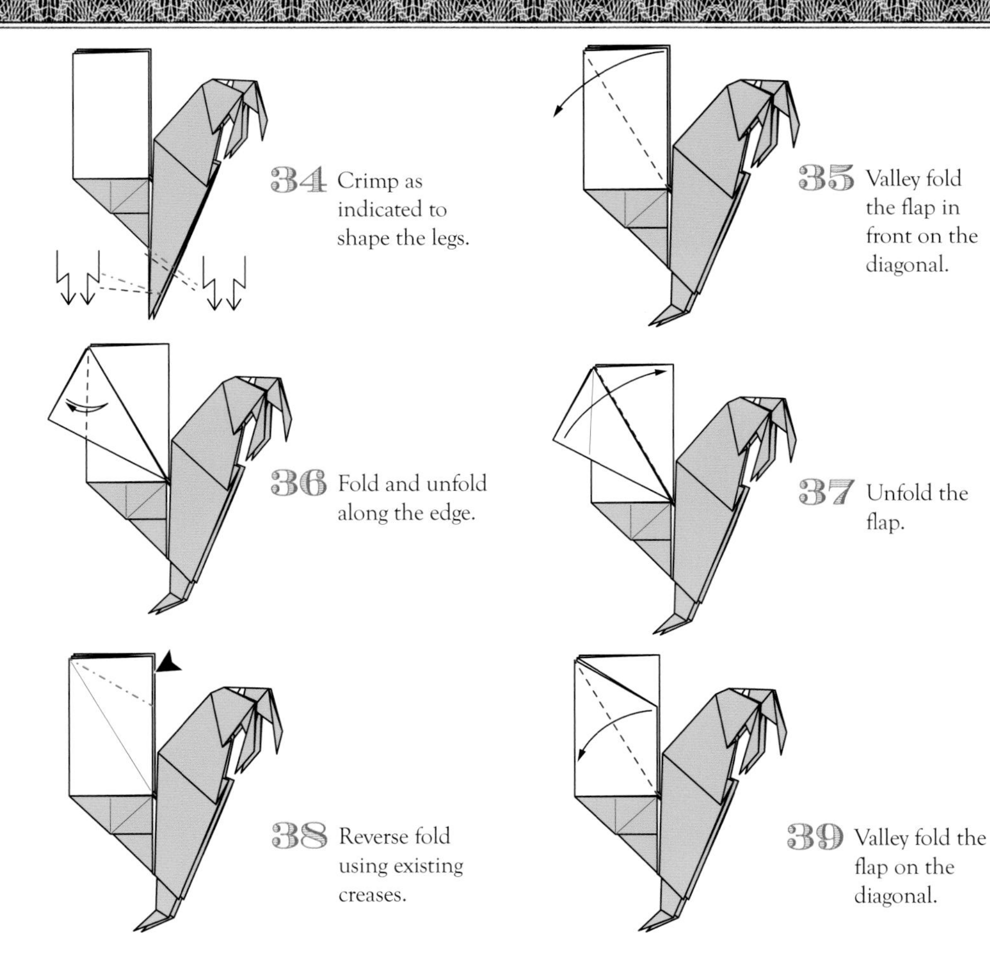

34 Crimp as indicated to shape the legs.

35 Valley fold the flap in front on the diagonal.

36 Fold and unfold along the edge.

37 Unfold the flap.

38 Reverse fold using existing creases.

39 Valley fold the flap on the diagonal.

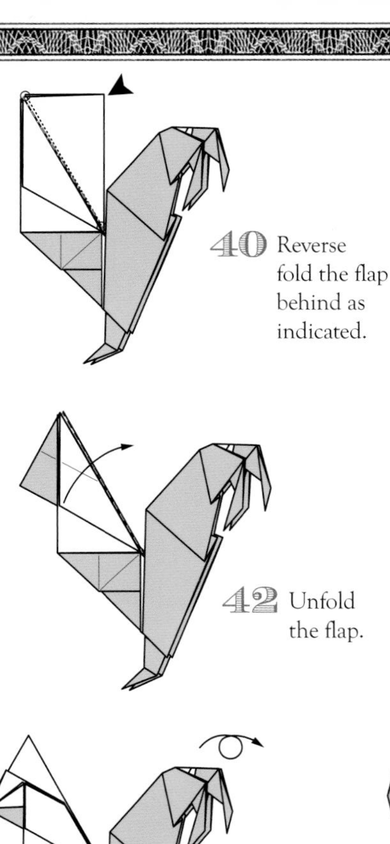

40 Reverse fold the flap behind as indicated.

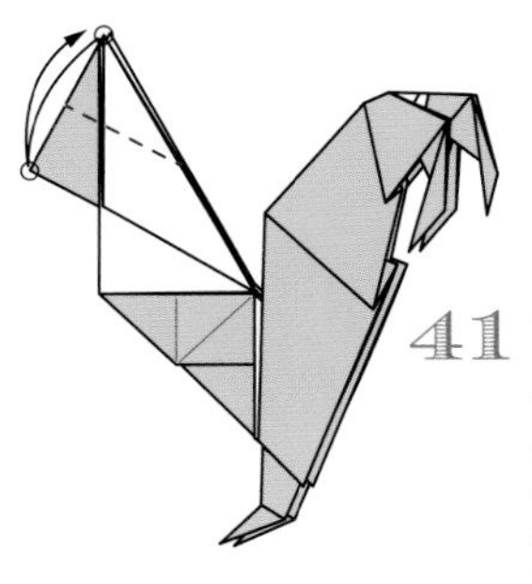

41 Fold the top corner to the lower corner. Crease well through all the layers. Unfold.

42 Unfold the flap.

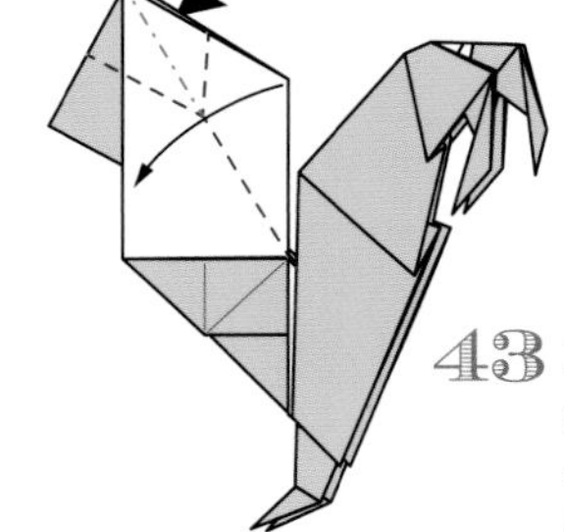

43 Reverse fold as indicated, using the creases formed in step 41.

44 Turn over.

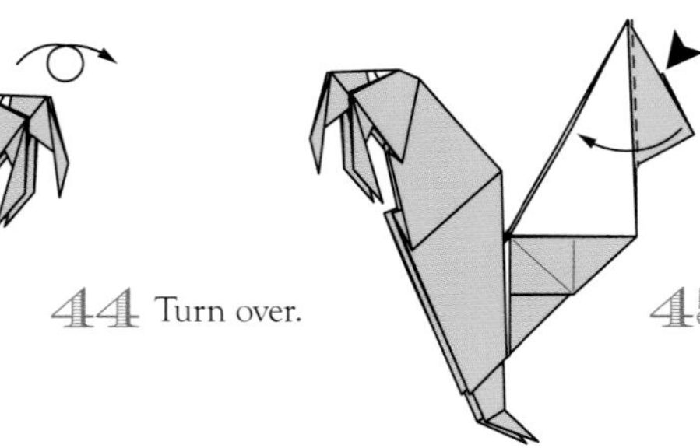

45 Valley fold the flap, squashing the corner behind it to flatten. See the next step for the result.

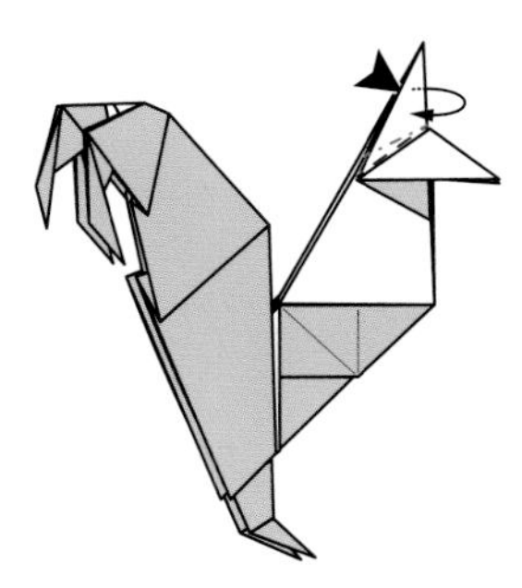

46 Open the flap, then twist and squash to shape the rooster's comb.

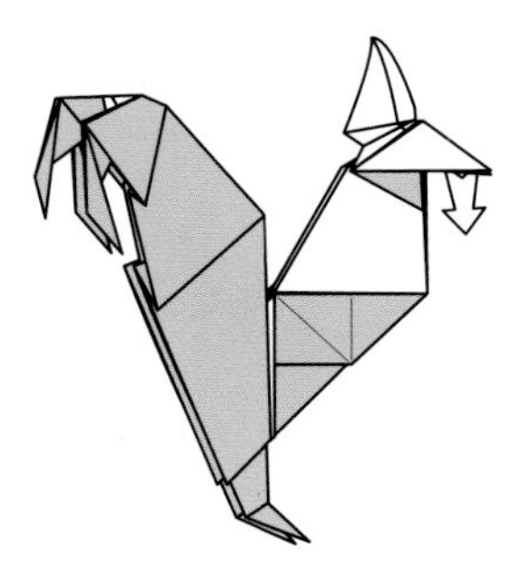

47 Open the beak.

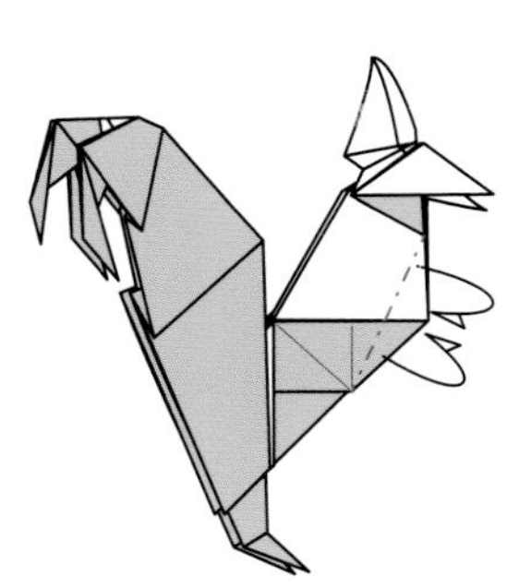

48 Fold the corners (front layer and back) to the inside.

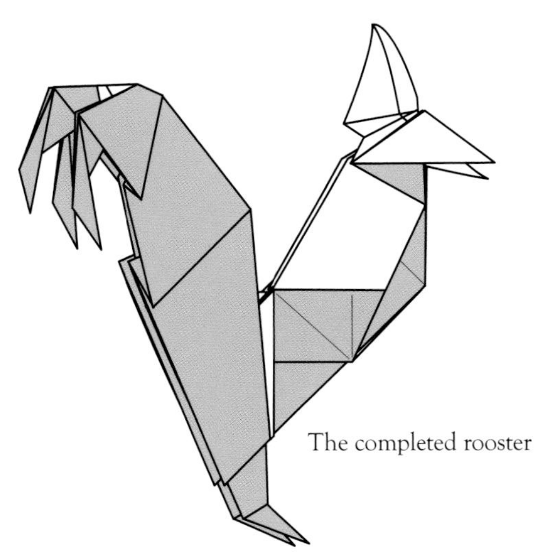

The completed rooster

TOUCH TONE TELEPHONE

You will need two bills to make this model.

Make the body of the phone first:

1 With the white (face) side up, fold in half. Unfold. Turn over.

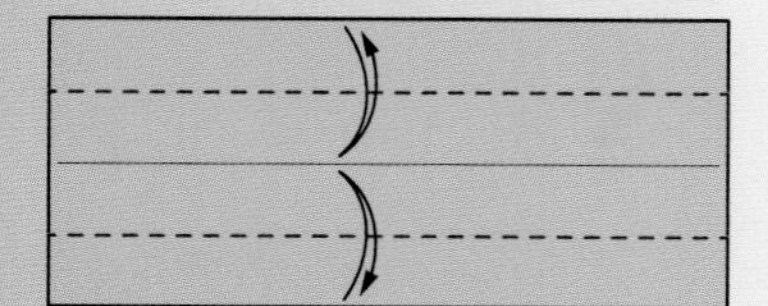

2 Fold in quarters. Unfold.

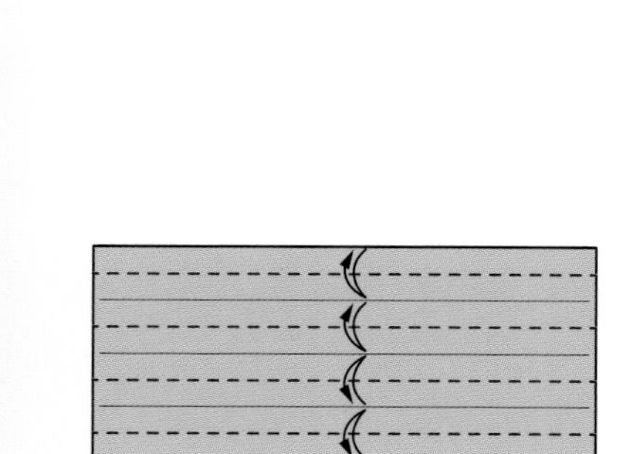

3 Fold in eighths. Unfold.

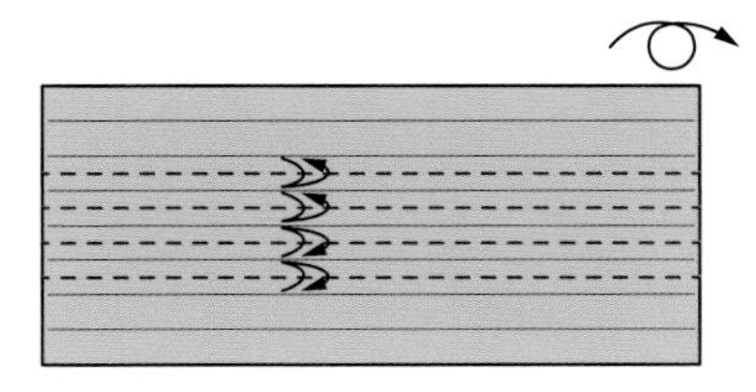

4 Fold between the creases as indicated. Unfold. Turn over.

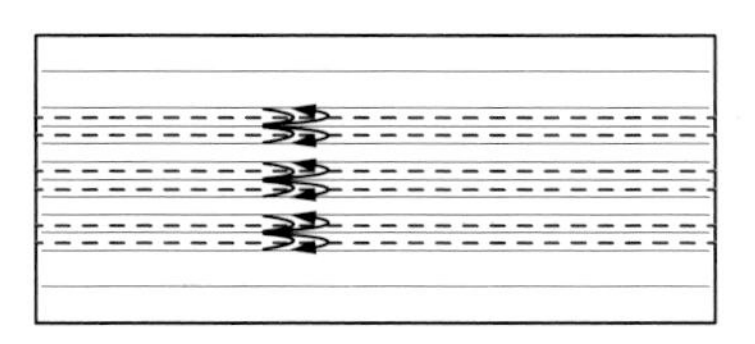

5 Crease between the creases as indicated. Unfold.

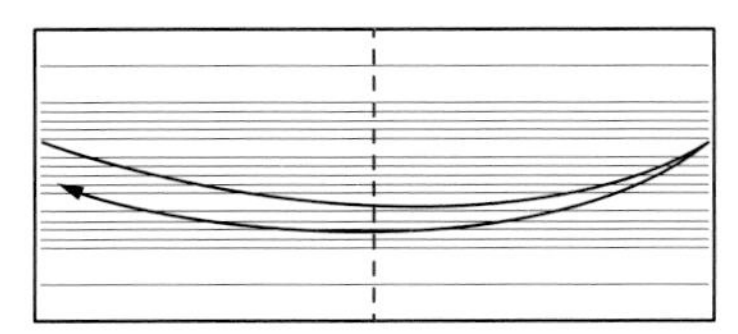

6 Fold in half. Unfold.

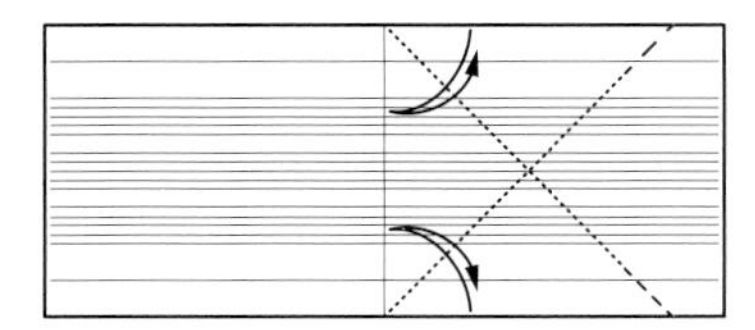

7 Fold on the diagonals, but crease only by the edges indicated.

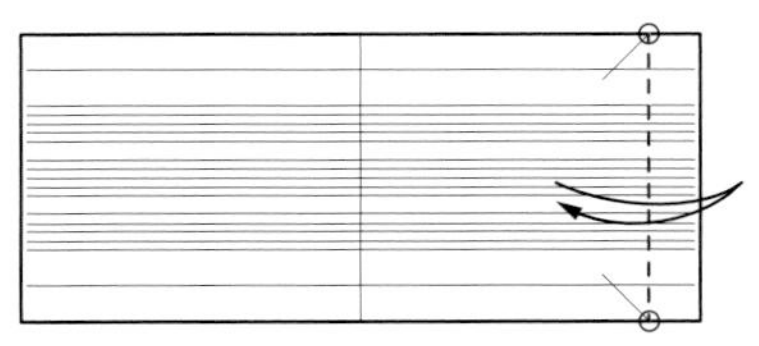

8 Fold between the reference points and unfold.

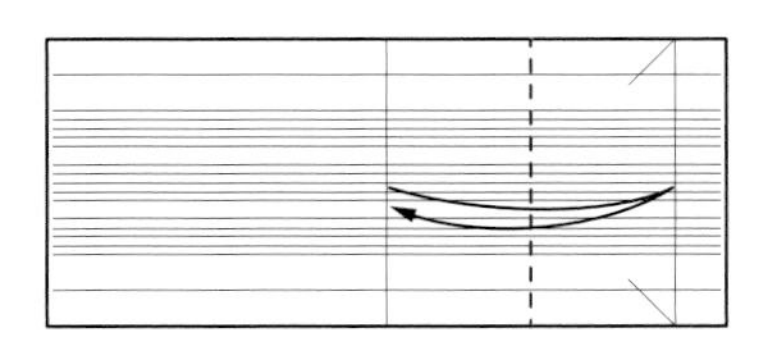

9 Valley fold crease to crease and unfold.

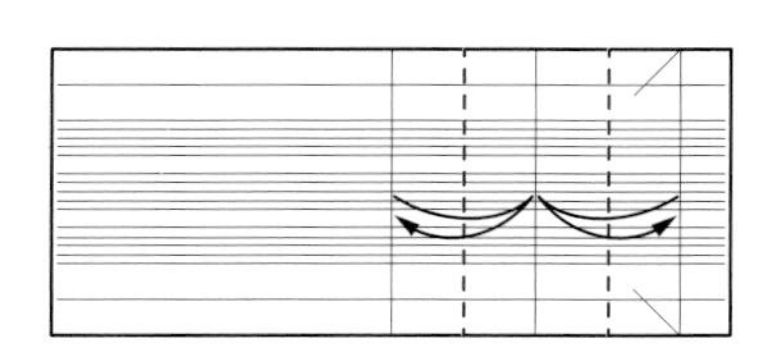

10 Crease between the creases. Unfold.

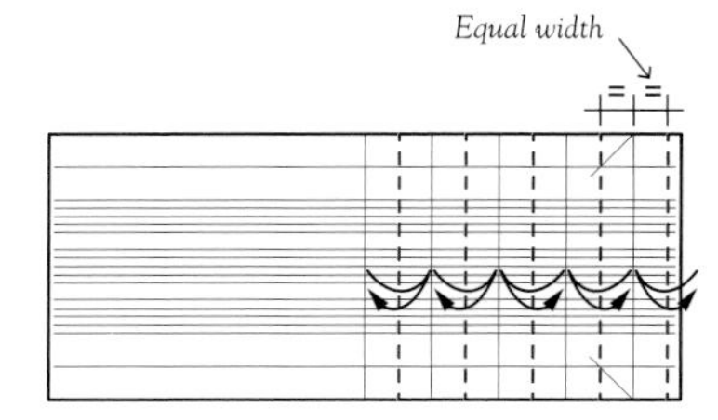

11 Crease between the creases. Note: Form a narrow flap on the far right edge to make another column the same width as the others.

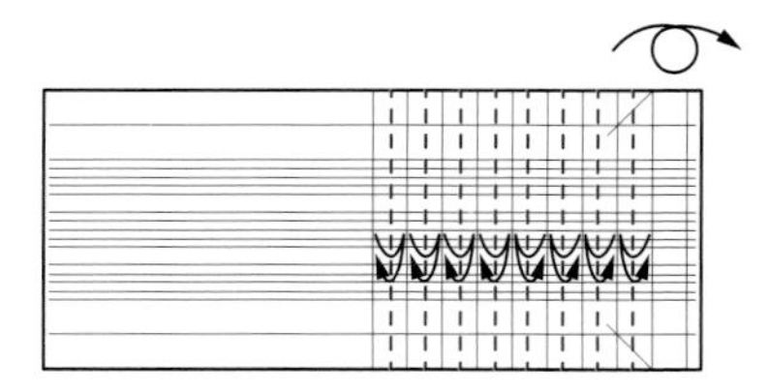

12 Crease between the creases. Turn over.

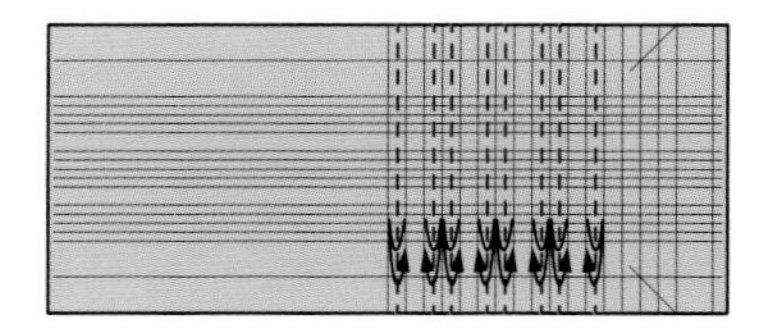

13 Crease between the creases.

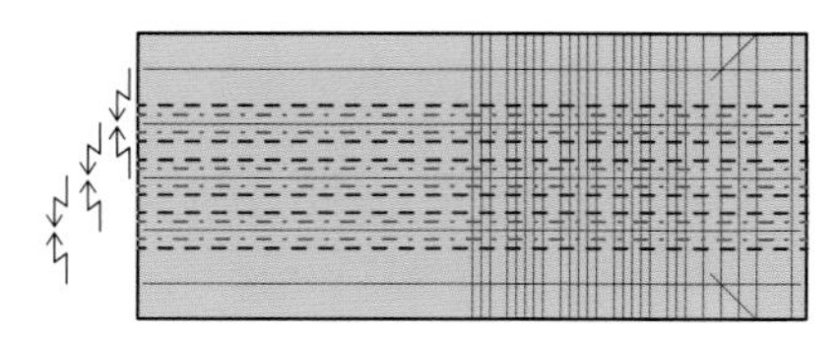

14 Fold a sequence of pleats as shown.

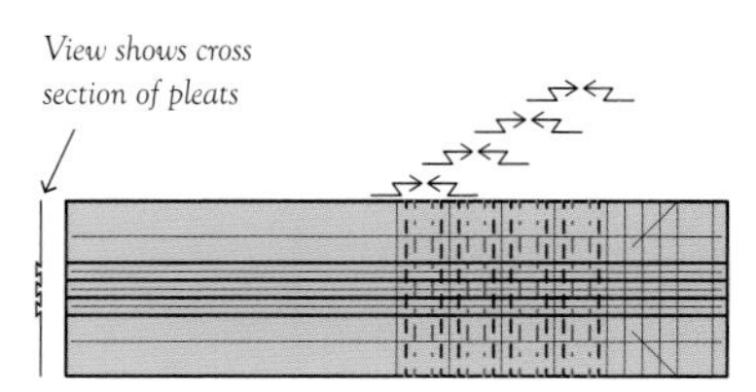

15 Fold another sequence of pleats perpendicular to the ones in step 14.

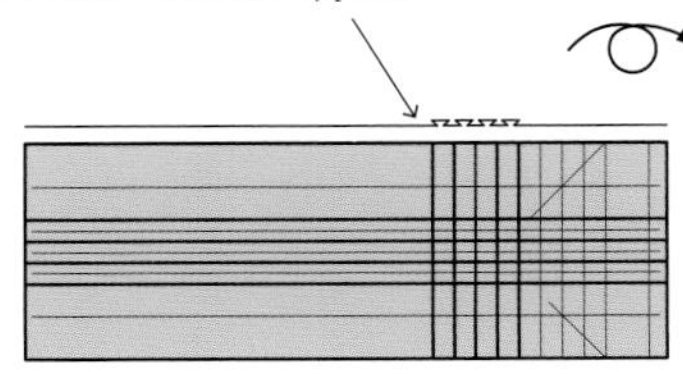

16 Turn over.

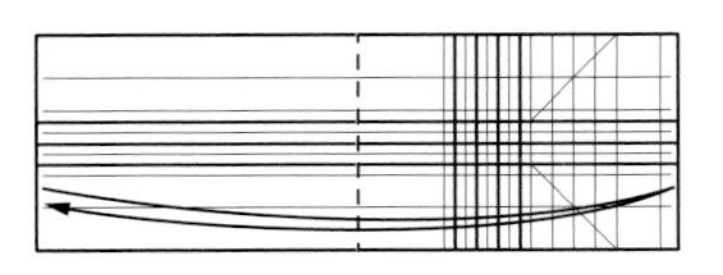

17 Fold in half. Unfold.

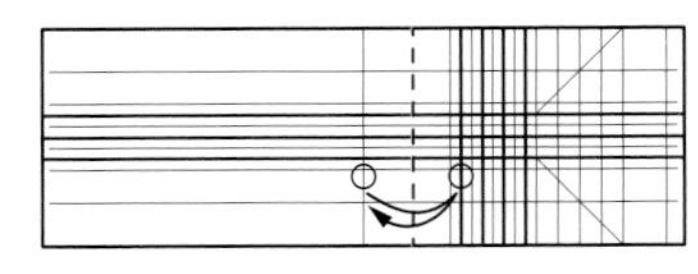

18 Fold the crease to the edge indicated. Unfold.

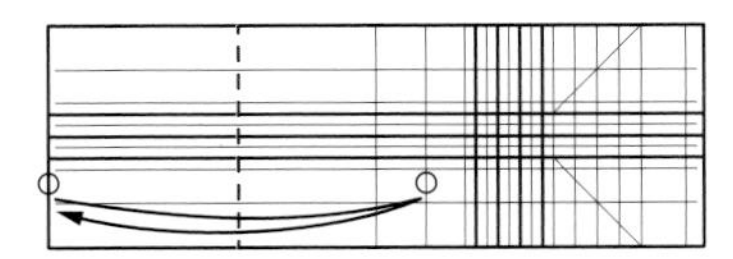

19 Fold the edge to the crease indicated. Unfold.

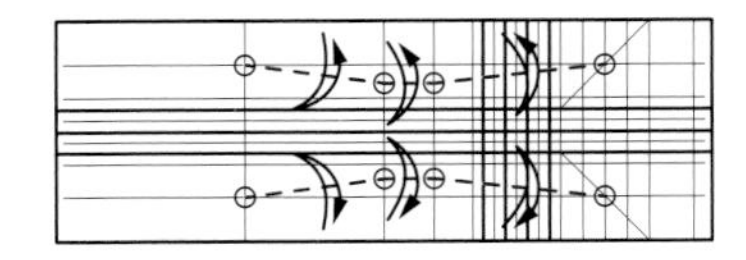

20 Valley fold between the reference points shown. Unfold.

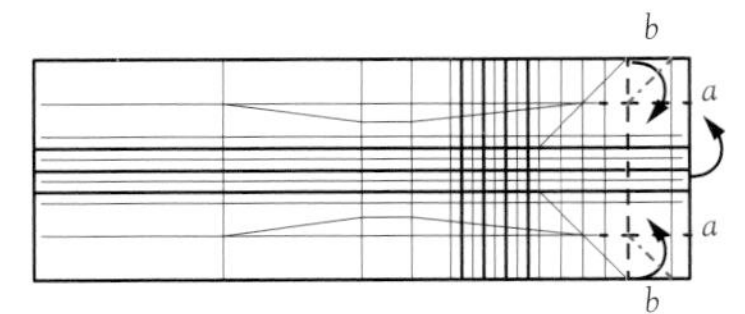

21 Make the model three-dimensional: Valley fold the edge into a U-shape (see *a* in diagram), then pleat the corners as if making a box (see *b* in diagram) so the flaps face the short side. The model will not lie flat.

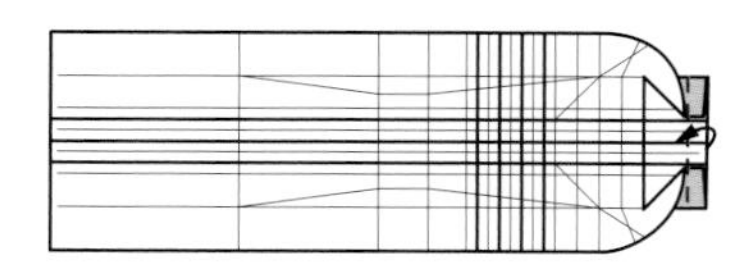

22 Valley fold the edge over to lock in place.

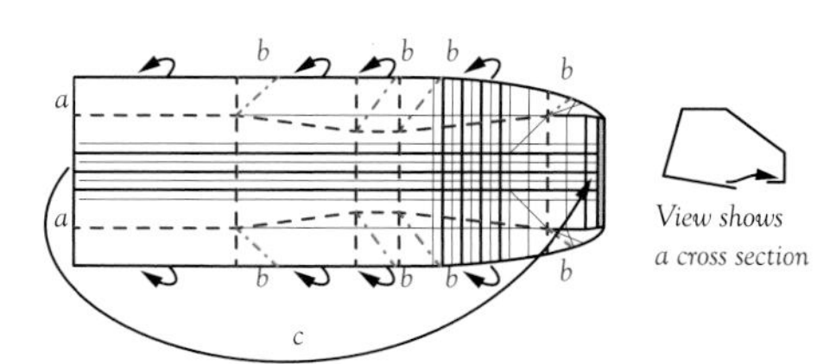

23 Valley fold the edges into a U-shape (see *a* in diagram), then create crimps to fold the body up (see *b* in diagram). Insert the left edge under the flap on the right, closing the unit (see *c* in diagram).

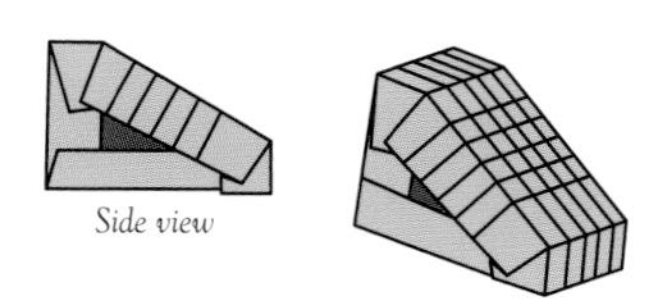

The finished phone body in side and ¾ view.

Use another bill to fold the handset:

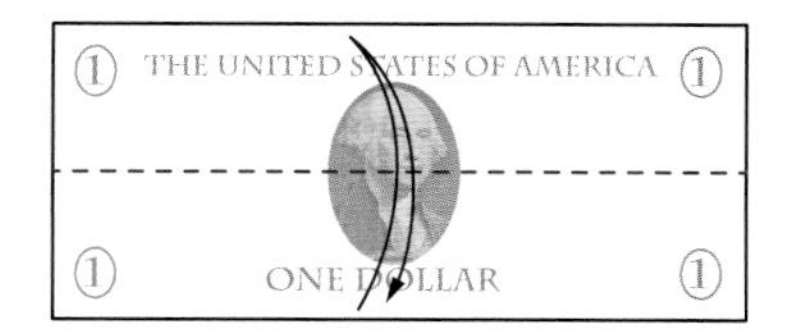

1 With the white (face) side up, fold in half. Unfold.

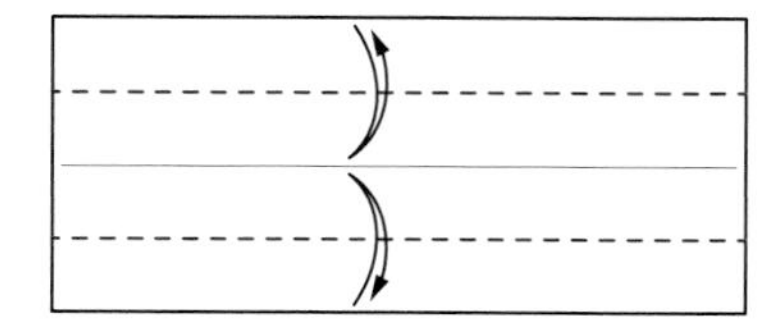

2 Fold in quarters. Unfold.

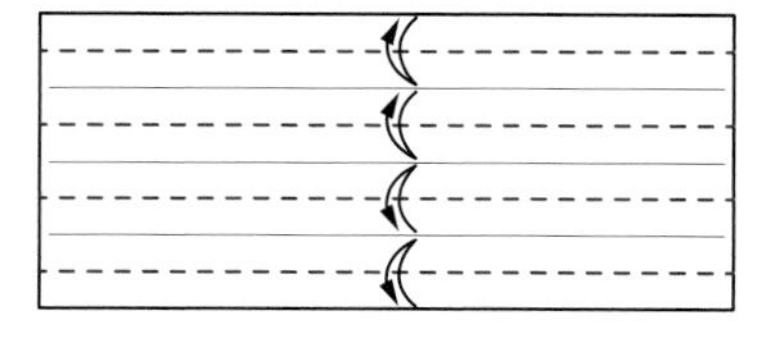

3 Fold in eighths. Unfold.

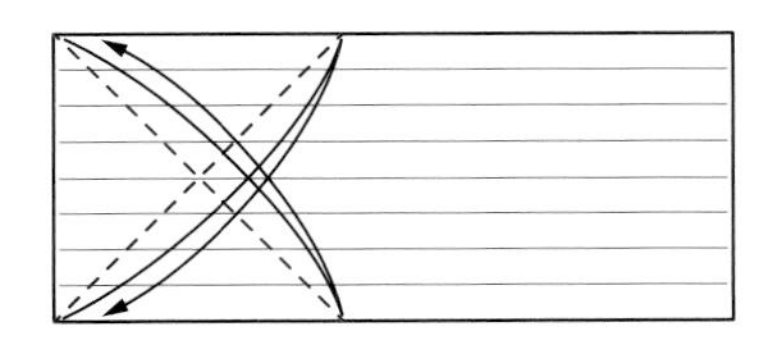

4 Fold the diagonals. Unfold.

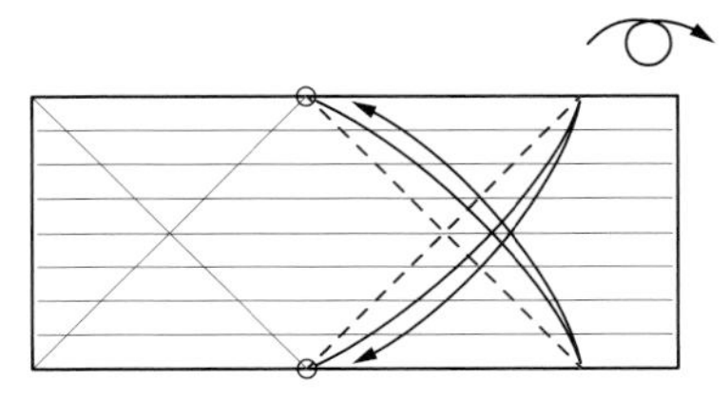

5 Fold the diagonals. Unfold. Turn over.

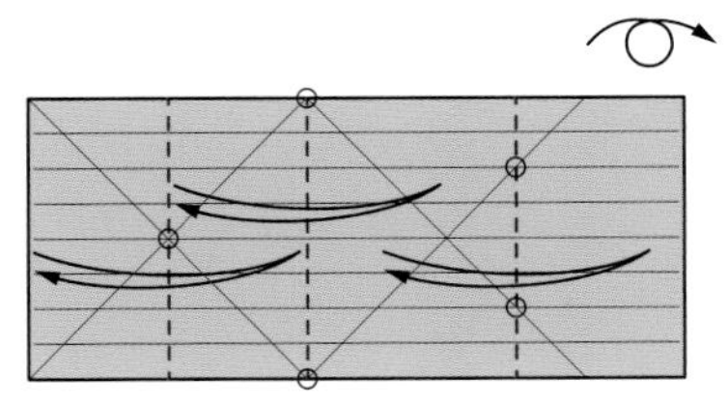

6 Form vertical creases through the intersection points shown. Turn over.

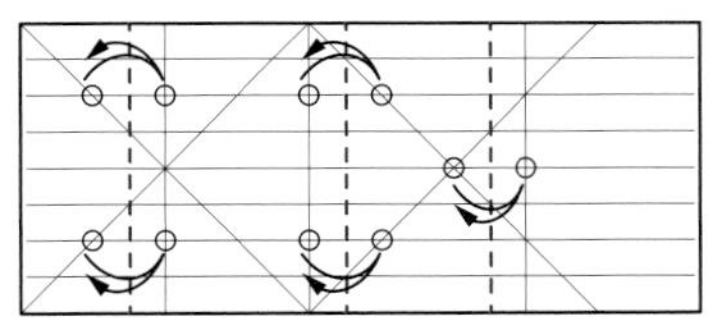

7 Fold reference points to reference points as shown, forming vertical creases.

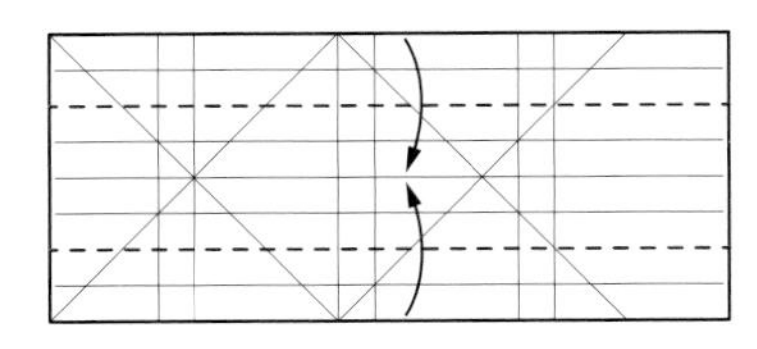

8 Fold the edges to the center.

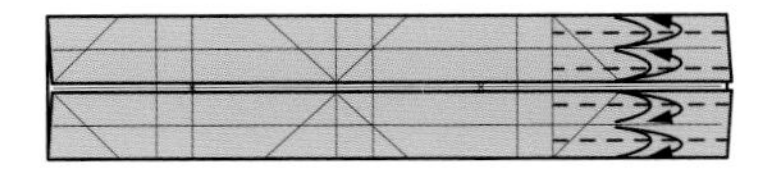

9 Valley fold as indicated. Unfold.

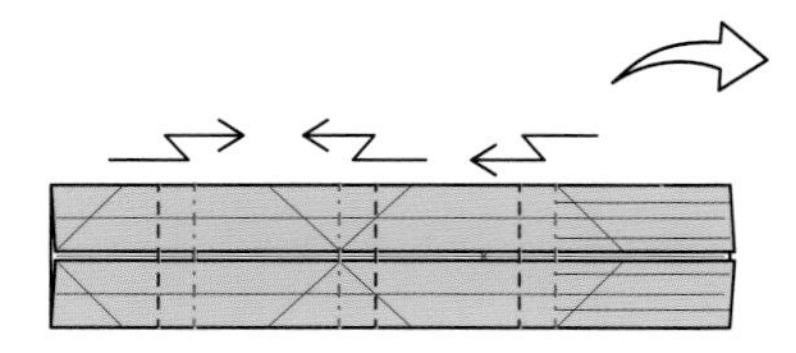

10 Pleat on existing creases.

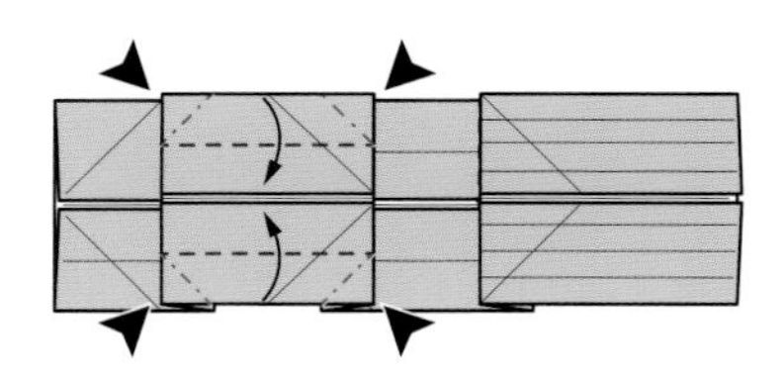

11 Valley fold the edges inward, squashing the corners.

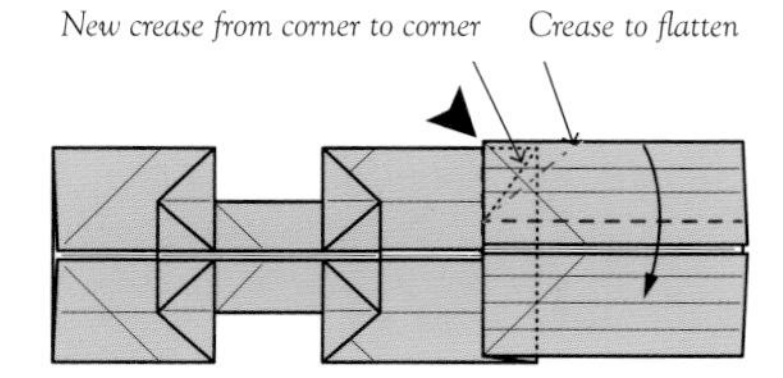

12 Valley fold on the existing crease, forming a new crease from corner to corner and flatten.

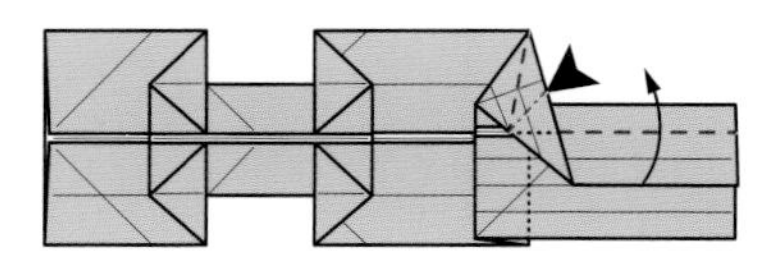

13 Valley fold on the existing crease, forming a new crease from corner to corner and flatten.

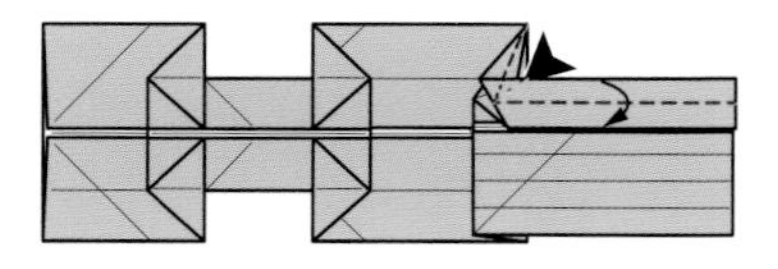

14 Valley fold on the existing crease, forming a new crease from corner to corner and flatten one last time.

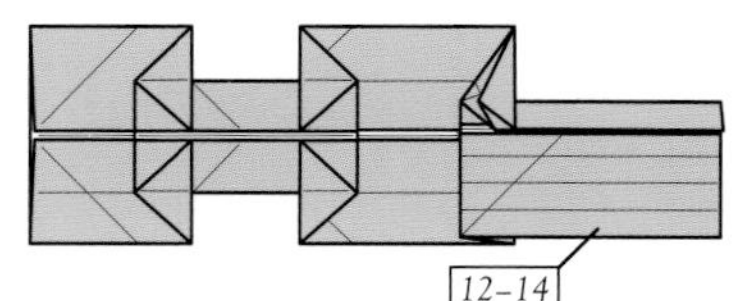

15 Repeat steps 12 to 14 on the other side.

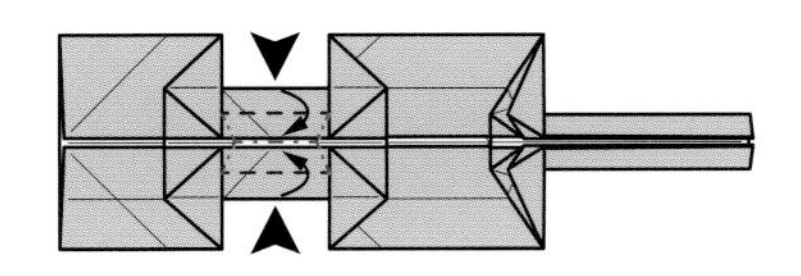

16 Make the center three-dimensional by folding the edges together to the center.

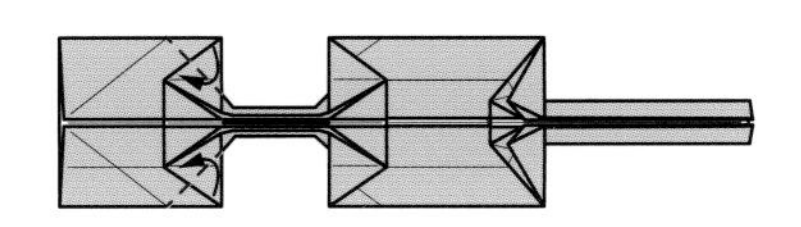

17 Valley fold the corners inward.

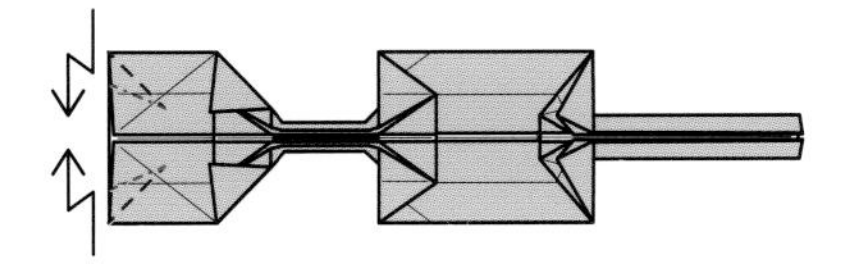

18 Pleat to make a concave shape.

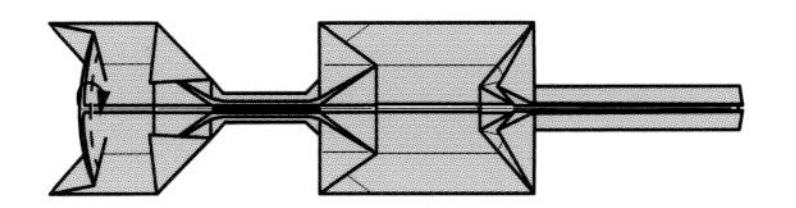

19 Valley fold the edge inside.

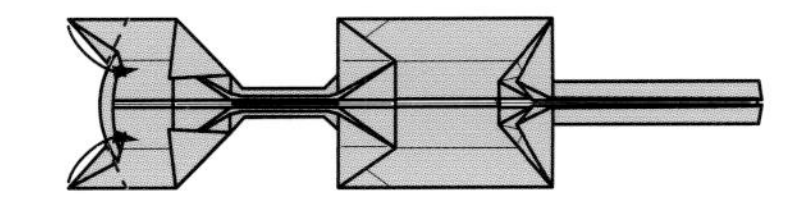

20 Fold the corners over to lock.

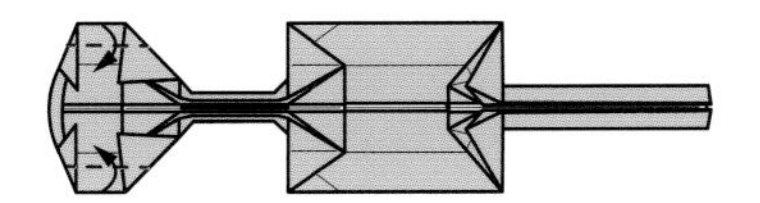

21 Valley fold the edges inside.

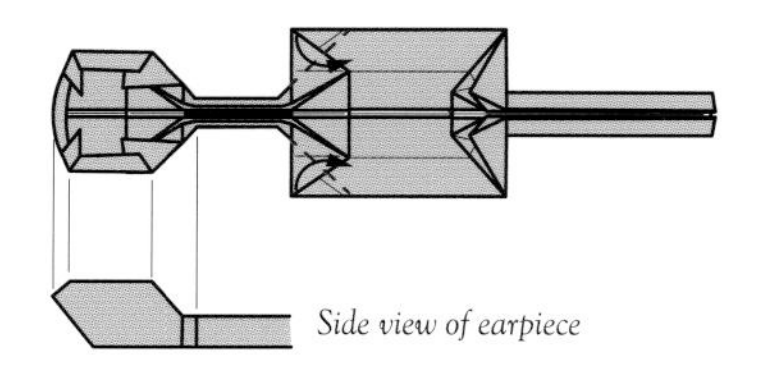

22 Valley fold the corners (as in step 17).

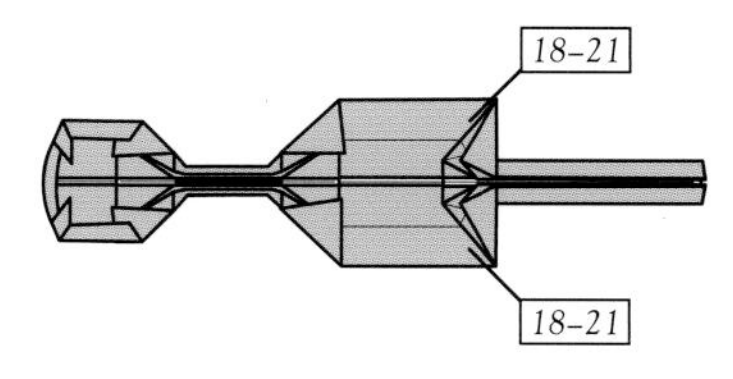

23 Repeat steps 18 to 21 on the corners indicated, skipping the valley fold shown in step 19.

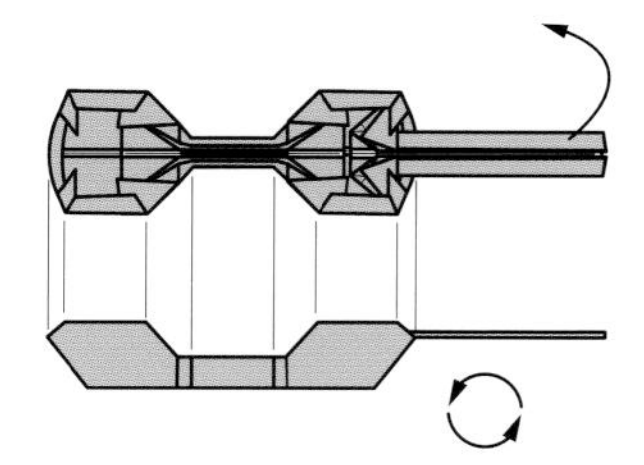

24 Curve the long flap to shape the cord. Rotate.

Assemble the pieces. Place the handset on top of the phone.

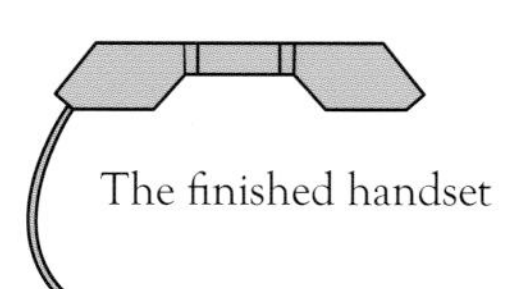

The finished handset

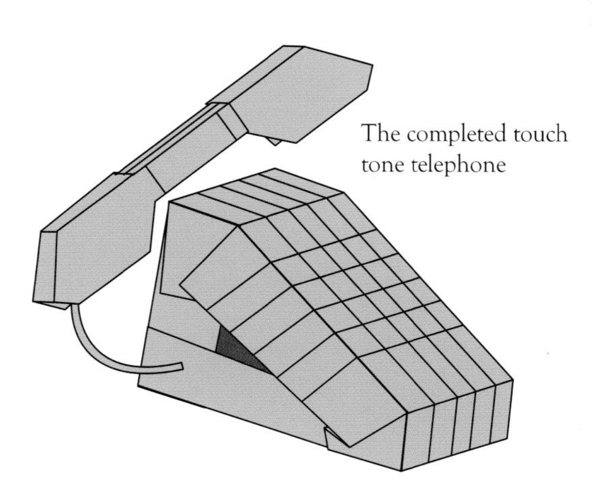

The completed touch tone telephone